NEW DIRECTIONS FOR ADULT AND CONTINUING EDUCATION

Ralph G. Brockett, *University of Tennessee, Knoxville*
EDITOR-IN-CHIEF

Alan B. Knox, *University of Wisconsin, Madison*
CONSULTING EDITOR

Applying Adult Development Strategies

Mark H. Rossman
Ottawa University

Maxine E. Rossman
Ottawa University

EDITORS

Number 45, Spring 1990

JOSSEY-BASS INC., PUBLISHERS
San Francisco • Oxford

Applying Adult Development Strategies.
Mark H. Rossman, Maxine E. Rossman (eds.).
New Directions for Adult and Continuing Education, no. 45.

NEW DIRECTIONS FOR ADULT AND CONTINUING EDUCATION
Ralph G. Brockett, Editor-in-Chief
Alan B. Knox, Consulting Editor

NEW DIRECTIONS FOR ADULT AND CONTINUING EDUCATION is part
of The Jossey-Bass Higher Education Series and is published
quarterly by Jossey-Bass Inc., Publishers (publication number
USPS 493-930). Second-class postage paid at San Francisco,
California, and at additional mailing offices. Postmaster: Send
address changes to Jossey-Bass Inc., Publishers, 350 Sansome
Street, San Francisco, California 94104.

EDITORIAL CORRESPONDENCE should be sent to the Editor-in-Chief,
Ralph G. Brockett, Dept. of Technological and Adult Education,
University of Tennessee, 402 Claxton Addition, Knoxville, Tennessee
37996-3400.

Library of Congress Catalog Card Number LC 85-644750

International Standard Serial Number ISSN 0195-2242

International Standard Book Number ISBN 1-55542-820-7

Photograph by Wernher Krutein/PHOTOVAULT.

Manufactured in the United States of America. Printed on acid-free paper

CONTENTS

Editors' Notes

More and more attention has been given in recent years to the application of adult development strategies. It is now recognized that adult development is not simply one long period lasting from the end of adolescence to the time of death but is a series of developmental periods dependent on a combination of social, biological, psychological, and physiological tasks and functions. This holistic view of adulthood not only has spurred new interest and research by and for educators of adults but also has generated new practices based on knowledge of adult development and learning. The purpose of this volume is to present an overview of adult development as well as several examples of strategies in action.

In Chapter One, Frederick Romero presents the theoretical framework for the book by providing a general overview of major adult development concepts in the areas of stage development, physiological development, and cognitive development.

In Chapter Two, Maxine E. Rossman and Mark H. Rossman present the Rossman Adult Learning Inventory (RALI), a forty-four-item tool designed to create an awareness of adult learning characteristics. They discuss the development of the RALI, provide sources for each item, and present techniques for using the RALI to create an awareness of adult learning characteristics and to change the way one teaches, counsels, advises, and learns.

Chapter Three presents a unique use of psychodrama. William D. Pearlman, a professional actor and psychologist, has pioneered the use of psychodrama as both a therapeutic exercise and a pedagogical format for understanding the dynamics of adult emotional and cognitive development.

Institutes of higher education need to be able to alter practice based on the developmental needs of the adult population. The highly innovative doctoral program of Walden University utilizes many of the concepts of adult development and learning and is presented by J. Bruce Francis in Chapter Four.

Equally innovative practices relating to higher education at the college level are presented in Chapters Five and Six. In Chapter Five, Daniel L. Foxx, Jr., provides an overview and rationale of the Proseminar, the initial course taken by adults returning to learning at Ottawa University. The course is designed to foster a supportive and noncompetitive environment based on the principles of adult learning. In Chapter Six, Callistus

W. Milan discusses the learning autobiography (LAB), a tool developed as part of the Proseminar at Ottawa University. The LAB assists the adult learner to assess strengths and weaknesses and encourages a mentoring relationship between the learner and the facilitator.

A problem faced by adults at every stage of development is stress. In Chapter Seven, Sybil A. McClary discusses stress and presents cogent ways the adult learner and adult educator can cope with and manage stress.

In Chapter Eight, Linda H. Lewis and Rosemary S. Caffarella conclude the volume by providing an annotation of selected current sources of information relating to adult development and learning.

This volume is based on the premise that to be most effective, adult educators must not only be aware of how adults develop throughout their postadolescent lifetimes but also able to translate this awareness into practical action. We hope that this volume demonstrates ways in which several practicing adult educators have made the transition from theory to practice.

Mark H. Rossman
Maxine E. Rossman
Editors

Mark H. Rossman is professor of education and director of graduate studies for the Phoenix Center of Ottawa University in Phoenix, Arizona. Formerly, he was acting chair of the Department of Higher and Adult Education at Arizona State University. He has written and lectured extensively on adult development and program development.

Maxine E. Rossman is professor of education and psychology at the Phoenix Center of Ottawa University in Phoenix, Arizona, where she works with adult learners seeking to complete their bachelor degrees. She has had a long-standing interest in adult experiential learning and currently serves on the regional staff of the Council for Adult and Experiential Learning.

Adult development is experienced by all but understood by relatively few.

Aspects of Adult Development

Frederick Romero

In the last two decades, a great deal of interest has focused on the special needs and characteristics of the emerging adult learner. Educators are seeking tested applications for teaching adults based on a variety of theories stemming from current research.

The interest in adult development has a long and distinguished history with researchers such as Erik Erikson and Abraham Maslow setting forth early theoretical assumptions concerning the progress of adults throughout their lives. Early researchers and scholars concerned with adult development came from a variety of professional backgrounds such as psychology, sociology, medicine, political science, and biology. Out of this foundation adult education, a relatively new professional discipline, emerged in the early 1960s. With the growing concern for adult educational opportunities in meeting the demands of an increasingly changing society, educators were faced with adult learners who brought with them different expectations and needs that did not fit the mold of younger students. This encouraged new research that added to the accepted assumptions of adult development and continues to increase our knowledge of the adult learner.

With the available research in contemporary adult education, practitioners have a wide variety of data and theories to investigate and possibly to add, dispute, or revise with their own findings (see Chapter Eight). However, adult educators must ultimately apply this accumulating knowledge in a structured setting. Applying theory to the learning environment is often difficult, and adding to this difficulty is the lack of available shared ideas and resources in educational techniques based on adult development theory.

NEW DIRECTIONS FOR ADULT AND CONTINUING EDUCATION, no. 45, Spring 1990 © Jossey-Bass Inc., Publishers

This chapter provides a general overview of major adult development concepts based on adult stage development, physiological development, and cognitive development. This overview will provide the reader with basic knowledge and a foundation on which to base the innovative, practical ideas that follow.

Stage Theory in Adult Development

Due to the limited scope of this summary, six major stage theorists were selected for review on the basis of both their impact on adult development theory and their diversity as a group. Pioneering ideas such as Erikson's stages have been incorporated with the ideas of more contemporary researchers such as Levinson and Perry.

Erik Erikson (1943) provides an eight-stage psychosocial development theory. Erikson, a trained Freudian psychoanalyst spurred by an interest in cultural anthropology, added to Freud's psychosexual stages of development by concentrating on social influences as well as on the psychologically maturing person. Erikson then continued from where Freud left off when he brought forth the innovative notion during the post-Freudian 1940s that people continue to develop through stages into late adulthood or old age. During this period adults are confronted with either a positive or negative resolution in each stage, which affects later stages.

Erikson begins his exploration of adult development in his sixth stage, which he labeled as the stage of intimacy versus isolation. Coming after the adolescent stage of identity versus identity confusion, this is the period in which the young adult seeks a sense of fulfillment not only through shared intimacy in friendships and love partners but also in developing affiliations with community and social groups or peers at work. There seems to be a need for acceptance, sharing, and belonging. If the young adult does not meet this need, a sense of isolation occurs in personal intimate relations and perhaps also in social, professional, or career relations.

As the adult reaches middle age, developmental needs may shift to what Erikson called generativity versus stagnation. To avoid a feeling of stunted growth, the person may develop a strong need to share knowledge and skills. Emphasis is placed on new priorities such as caring for others, getting involved in civic duties, and becoming more creative and productive. The adult feels a sense of enrichment when opportunities arise that allow expression of personal experience, values, ideas, and philosophy through teaching, guiding, or supervising. The self-centered individual who is concerned only with personal needs may develop a sense of stagnation, distorted perceptions, and lack of caring.

Finally, in older age, the adult encounters the resolution of integrity versus despair. When the adult feels at peace with lifelong accomplishments and has adapted to both success and failure, a sense of integrity can develop. Associated with this integrity the adult develops what is best described as wisdom. Wisdom brings to the older adult a level of peace and confidence enabling detachment from many needs of past stages. Perhaps wisdom and integrity can also lead to new and exciting directions in a person's life even as he or she faces the inevitability of death.

Robert J. Havighurst (1972) viewed developmental tasks of adulthood as meeting the needs of the individual in context with what society considers healthy growth and success. Havighurst informs us that developmental tasks of early adulthood center on priorities dealing with finding a mate and, once found, learning to live with this mate, starting a family and managing a home, getting started in a career, taking civic responsibility, and finding a suitable social group. After a great deal of study of adults between the ages of forty and seventy, Havighurst arrived at a set of developmental directions for the middle-aged person. These directions are mental flexibility versus rigidity, emotional expansion versus constriction, expansion of interests beyond the work role, valuing wisdom versus valuing physical power, and body transcendence versus body preoccupation (Long, 1983). These directions are the foundation for developmental tasks that Havighurst identified as achieving civic and social responsibility, establishing an economic standard of living, assisting adolescents in their development into adulthood, developing leisure activities, coping with physiological changes, adjusting to aging parents, and relating to one's spouse as a person.

Havighurst provides insights into learning motivation that are relevant to the education of adults. In his theory of the "teachable moment" the adult senses great urgency as a developmental task becomes important. This creates a high degree of motivation to learn new behaviors in order to meet task demands (Long, 1983). During this motivation period, instruction can have a high degree of effectiveness and impact on the adult learner.

William Perry (1970), as a result of an intensive study of eighty-four Harvard undergraduate students, established nine developmental positions based on the students' experiences through the college years. In Perry's model, learners perceive the world in "absolutist" terms in the first three positions. In the first position, students view the world in polar terms of right and wrong, good and bad, and we and others. Those in authority are seen as having the role of teaching absolute truth to the student. The student begins to perceive different opinions and uncertainty in the second position, which may be blamed on instructor competence or exercises established by authority so the "truth" may be found. In the third position the student accepts diversity and uncertainty as legitimate but temporary in cases where authority has not yet found the answers.

The learner begins to allow for diversity and the problematical nature of life in position four, when legitimate uncertainty is perceived. This perception develops into the belief in position five that all knowledge and values are contextual and relativistic. In position six the learner realizes that it is necessary to orient to a relativistic world through personal commitment. Finally, in the last three positions, learners find their own place in a relativistic world through personal commitment. In position seven the learner makes an initial commitment in a given area, which evolves into experiencing the implications of the commitment. In positions eight and nine the learner experiences the affirmation of identity and realizes commitment as an ongoing activity through which lifestyles are expressed (Cross, 1981).

The positions established by Perry are not rigidly sequential, and they do not include all the variables in adult learning since they are based on interviews with younger undergraduate students. However, they do provide a useful analytical structure in understanding the development of critical reflectivity in adults (Brookfield, 1986). Perry found that most Harvard freshmen enter college at positions three through five and graduate in positions six through eight. Although position nine was rarely observed in younger college students, it may be more common in adult learners (Cross, 1981).

Brookfield (1986) summarizes Perry's contribution quite well:

> The Perry scheme represents an interesting area of future speculation for theorists of adult learning. Perry's contribution has been to posit an initial framework in which the transition from dualism to relativism to critically aware commitment has been clearly outlined. If these stages can be translated into specific outcomes, with sufficient flexibility of interpretation so that widely varying settings can be included, this might provide adult teachers with a means by which they could recognize the diversity of stages reached by different members of learning groups. Alternatively, and in a more inductive manner, the framework provides an analytical construct that one can apply to many different educational initiatives as a way of coming to understand the teaching-learning transactions occurring therein [p. 145].

Adults bring to the learning environment knowledge based on past experiences in professions and personal development, which probably have influenced their values and moral or ethical beliefs. Since an individual's sense of morality is the foundation from which attitudes, beliefs, and personal goals derive and in turn affect learning, moral sensibility is an important variable to consider.

Lawrence Kohlberg (Kohlberg and Turiel, 1971) established his cognitive-developmental stage theory based on a moral development model.

Kohlberg theorizes that a child begins development in a premoral stage in which there is a lack of perceptual understanding of rules and authority. From this "zero" stage the child develops to the preconventional level, consisting of stage one (dealing with punishment and obedience) and stage two (where satisfying one's needs through appropriate action is the priority). The child may appropriately respond to rules but is motivated by consequences such as reward, punishment, or exchange of favors. Moving to the conventional level, the individual learns in stage three that appropriate or good behavior is socially approved. In stage four, the law-and-order orientation develops. At this level, conformity to social expectations becomes valuable and a sense of loyalty to maintain the social order is exhibited. Finally, at the postconventional level, personal values and principles apart from social or group expectations begin to be explored and defined. A sense of autonomy becomes important here, in stage five, as individual rights and opinions are stressed as long as social standards are maintained. The legal point of view is emphasized but only under the option of changing laws under a democratic consensus based on individual rights and opinions. In stage six the universal-ethical-principle orientation emerges. Abstract beliefs such as universal human rights, equality, dignity, and justice are strengthened. Respect for individual dignity becomes the foundation for this final stage in Kohlberg's theory (Cross, 1981).

Loevinger (1976) examined development in terms of personality characteristics through extensive clinical studies. From her research, Loevinger established what she identifies as milestones of ego development. The stages in ego development are identified as presocial, symbiotic, impulsive, self-protective, conformist, conscientious-conformist, conscientious, individualistic, autonomous, and integrated. According to Loevinger, each stage has characteristics dealing with character development, interpersonal style, conscious preoccupations, and cognitive style.

Because each stage influences personality and thinking, as one progresses viewpoints and perceptions may change as the individual matures or develops from the lower-level stages to higher levels of ego development. This can be illustrated by responses to Loevinger's use of a thirty-six-item projective test involving sentence completion. Responses to completing the item on education indicated that people at the lower-level stages viewed education as a "thing" one gets in school and then owns. At the conformist stage, education is viewed for its practical usefulness, which is necessary for citizens and essential for good careers. Attitudes become different at the conscientious stage, where education is viewed as important for personal enrichment and valuable to society. During the autonomous stage, education is considered an ongoing process that leads to creativity, strengthened values, and personal fulfillment (Cross, 1981).

There continues to be a need for investigation in developmental stages. Erikson and Havighurst developed their stage theories in the 1950s. During this period traditional cultural values were prevalent. As examinations of the roles of adults revealed, these values influenced priorities in various stages. Current and future adult developmental theories must address such phenomena as changing attitudes toward career shifts, including educational needs that concern job obsolescence and women's new roles in the work force, and coping with changing family values.

Physical Development

Generally, physical strength and most bodily functions peak when a person is in her or his twenties, then gradually decline. The eyes are usually the first organs to change with age. Visual acuity is at its best at around eighteen to twenty years of age, with a slow steady decline until the age of forty, at which time decline noticeably increases. Between the ages of forty-five and fifty-five, the adult experiences the most striking change. Symptoms include a decrease in focus ability, decrease in peripheral vision, sensitivity to glare, and slower adjustment to the dark (Cross, 1981; Rossman, Fisk, and Roehl, 1984).

Hearing loss is another problem encountered by the older adult. Generally, peak hearing is reached before the age of fifteen. After hearing ability peaks, there is a steady, gradual decline until about age sixty-five, with the most marked decrease starting after age forty-five (Rossman, Fisk, and Roehl, 1984).

Hearing loss impairs the adult's ability to discriminate among sounds, which may result in speech discrimination impairment. The adult educator may need to compensate for this problem by speaking slowly, distinctly, and with sufficient volume. Shorter sentences should be used, since hearing loss reduces the ability to recall long sentences (Rossman, Fisk, and Roehl, 1984).

Physical decline may not be as important to the learning environment as the psychological damage that may result (for example, loss of confidence, frustration, and anxiety). With determination the adult learner can easily overcome a decrease in physical abilities and perform exceptionally well in a learning situation. However, all too often adults have difficulty overcoming emotional distress and lack of confidence. These potential problems can be effectively dealt with when the educator is cognizant of them and establishes an optimal learning environment and delivery to help compensate for both the physical and the psychological problems.

Cognitive Development

Intelligence was once believed to reach its peak around the ages of eighteen to twenty-one and then to decline. Into the 1960s, researchers believed that creative abilities also declined after peaking between the ages of twenty and forty (Biehler and Hudson, 1986). These conclusions were largely based on cross-sectional studies dealing with samples of different age groups and their performance level on IQ tests. Because of these beliefs, there was little interest in measuring adult intelligence. This early notion of intelligence and creativity does not hold up to modern findings.

One significant problem of cross-sectional designs was the methodology used. The IQ tests used in the studies were timed tests rather than power tests. Older individuals tend to be more cautious and deliberate in their actions and do not respond to speed test requirements as well as do younger individuals (Birren, Woods, and Williams, 1980).

Results of longitudinal studies show only slight declines of intelligence based on age. In fact, longitudinal studies generally conclude that there is a rise in intelligence until the mid-forties (Biehler and Hudson, 1986). There are still mixed results when the data from longitudinal and cross-sectional studies are compared, and both techniques exhibit methodological problems. Most contemporary researchers are more interested in investigating various forms of cognitive functions over differences in IQ scores based on chronological age (Cross, 1981). One area in cognitive abilities that has produced a great deal of interest is the examination of crystallized and fluid intelligence.

Crystallized intelligence refers to abilities learned through both formal and informal experience. *Fluid intelligence* is based on constitutional factors such as memory, creativity, and cognitive style (Horn and Cattell, 1967; Biehler and Hudson, 1986). Evidence indicates that fluid intelligence, being dependent on neurological efficiency, reaches a peak in the twenties, then declines. Crystallized intelligence, however, increases as fluid intelligence decreases. Crystallized intelligence is augmented as the individual gains in experience over the maturing process, which also develops increased problem-solving abilities (Cross, 1981; Biehler and Hudson, 1986). Often these abilities are referred to as "wisdom."

Although memory is thought to decline with age, there is general agreement among researchers that the deterioration is minor until old age. Aging has somewhat more impact on the time needed to learn new things. Although there are substantial individual differences, generally older adults need more time to perceive stimuli prior to reacting (Cross, 1981). When the pace of learning is controlled, most adults in their forties and fifties have the same ability to learn as they had in their twenties and thirties (Knox, 1977).

Cross (1981) describes the difference between fluid and crystallized intelligence in the context of the adult learner:

> In the literature of adult education, it is common to speak of older people's "compensating" for the loss of quickness in learning by substitut-

ing experience and wisdom, but Schaie and Parr (1981) advance the thesis that different stages of life actually call for different learning abilities. Youth is the time for acquisition, young adulthood the time for achievement, middle age the time for responsibility, and old age the time for reintegration. These phases of the life cycle call for different kinds of learning abilities. Most school learning, with its emphasis on acquisition rather than application or responsibility, is designed to capitalize on the learning strengths of young people. Both the methods and the content of traditional schooling are disadvantageous to older learners, who would, according to the research, perform better on tasks calling for crystallized intelligence. The educational model that would capitalize on the learning strengths of adults would deemphasize the processing and acquisition of large amounts of new information, emphasizing instead the development of cognitive functions calling for integration, interpretation, and application of knowledge. Speed and quickness in learning would also give way to emphasis on responsibility and accuracy [p. 162].

Conclusion

Today the adult educator has access to thousands of annual reports investigating adult learning. However, there are still many questions to be answered before adult education becomes a science (Long, 1983). Researchers and educators of adults will need to provide information on the best forms of delivery in the learning environment and determine the needed competence of the adult learning facilitator.

To learn what techniques are best utilized in adult learning and what the facilitator needs to bring to the learning process, a careful review of current techniques and facilitator attitudes and knowledge based on what is known about adult developmental theory is warranted.

References

Biehler, R. F., and Hudson, L. M. *Developmental Psychology: An Introduction.* Boston: Houghton Mifflin, 1986.
Birren, J. E., Woods, A. M., and Williams, M. V. "Behavioral Slowing with Age: Causes, Organization, and Consequences." In L. W. Poon (ed.), *Aging in the 1980's.* Washington, D.C.: American Psychological Association, 1980.
Brookfield, S. D. *Understanding and Facilitating Adult Learning: A Comprehensive Analysis of Principles and Effective Practices.* San Francisco: Jossey-Bass, 1986.
Cross, K. P. *Adults as Learners: Increasing Participation and Facilitating Learning.* San Francisco: Jossey-Bass, 1981.
Erikson, E. H. *Childhood and Society.* New York: Norton, 1943.
Havighurst, R. J. *Developmental Tasks and Education.* New York: McKay, 1972.
Horn, J. L., and Cattell, R. B. "Age Differences in Fluid and Crystallized Intelligence." *Acta Psychologica*, 1967, *26*, 107–129.

Knox, A. B. *Adult Development and Learning: A Handbook on Individual Growth and Competence in the Adult Years*. San Francisco: Jossey-Bass, 1977.

Kohlberg, L., and Turiel, E. "Moral Development and Moral Education." In G. S. Lesser (ed.), *Psychology and Educational Practice*. Glenview, Ill.: Scott, Foresman, 1971.

Loevinger, J. *Ego Development: Concepts and Theories*. San Francisco: Jossey-Bass, 1976.

Long, H. B. *Adult Learning: Research and Practice*. New York: Cambridge University Press, 1983.

Perry, W. G., Jr. *Forms of Intellectual and Ethical Development in the College Years*. New York: Holt, Rinehart & Winston, 1970.

Rossman, M. H., Fisk, E. C., and Roehl, J. E. *Teaching and Learning Basic Skills: A Guide for Adult Basic Education and Developmental Education Programs*. New York: Teachers College Press, 1984.

Schaie, K. W., and Parr, J. "Intelligence." In A. W. Chickering and Associates (eds.), *The Modern American College: Responding to the New Realities of Diverse Students and a Changing Society*. San Francisco: Jossey-Bass, 1981.

Frederick Romero is assistant professor of psychology for Ottawa University in Phoenix, Arizona.

To change teaching, counseling, advising, or learning styles,
it is necessary to understand adult learning characteristics and
their implications.

The Rossman Adult Learning Inventory: Creating Awareness of Adult Development

Maxine E. Rossman, Mark H. Rossman

The literature is replete with books, chapters, monographs, and articles concerned with adult development (see Chapters One and Eight). All too often neither the educators of adults nor the adult learners themselves have an extensive awareness of this information, or a tool to determine the extent to which this knowledge is known or understood.

Background. In 1977, as part of a doctoral dissertation, a sixty-item questionnaire, the Rossman Adult Learning Inventory (RALI), was conceptualized, developed, field-tested, and revised (Rossman, 1977). The purpose of the study was to determine the extent to which community college faculty were aware of adult learning characteristics.

The questionnaire segments adult development characteristics into four sections: (1) orientation to learning, (2) mental abilities, (3) physiological factors, and (4) psychological factors. Each item on the RALI is supported by research in the field of adult education and development.

Since its inception, the RALI and supporting documentation have been presented formally in a variety of institutional settings in the United States, Europe, and Asia. The RALI has also been introduced in many staff development workshops and university adult education classes. Subsequent use of the RALI over the years has led to its refinement based on experience, current literature, and research.

The Instrument. In 1989, as a result of revisions, a forty-four-item version of the RALI, utilizing the same four categories as in the original RALI was developed. The revised version of the RALI, together with its correct answers and a source summary, is presented in Exhibits 1 and 2 of this chapter.

Administration of the RALI

Before administering the RALI, the facilitator must be familiar not only with the inventory shown in Exhibit 1, but also with the source summaries given in Exhibit 2.

The RALI can be administered to groups of various sizes. The administration and discussion of the RALI take about one to two hours.

Exhibit 1. The Rossman Adult Learning Inventory

Directions: The following list contains a series of general statements about the characteristics of the adult learner (over twenty-five years of age). If you think the statement is true, put a T in the blank. If you think the statement is false, put an F in the blank. Please answer each question.

_____ 1. Adult learners should be encouraged to relate new or difficult concepts to their existing experience.

_____ 2. Adult learners are often issue (or problem) centered rather than subject centered.

_____ 3. It is difficult for an adult to do a familiar task in an unfamiliar way.

_____ 4. Adult learners usually want educational experiences that relate to job/ life situations.

_____ 5. Most adult learning occurs outside formal education institutions.

_____ 6. An adult's experience may interfere with the learning process.

_____ 7. Adult learners should not be involved in formulating their learning objectives.

_____ 8. Adult learners desire minimum time expenditures to complete their educational objectives.

_____ 9. Adults and children have the same orientation to learning.

_____ 10. There is very little diversity in groups of adult learners.

_____ 11. Adult students should not be allowed to set their own learning pace.

_____ 12. The pattern of mental abilities does not change with age.

_____ 13. Performance of adults on tests measuring vocabulary and general information improves with age.

_____ 14. Compared to youth, adults usually require a longer time to perform learning tasks.

_____ 15. Age influences the speed of learning.

_____ 16. Age in itself does little to affect an individual's power to learn.

_____ 17. Adult learning is influenced by the amount of previous formal education.

_____ 18. Scores on tests measuring dexterity show no decline with age.

_____ 19. Motivation of the adult taking a test is not a major factor in performance.

_____ 20. Recency of participation in an educational activity improves an adult's educational performance.

_____ 21. All adult students have the same learning style.

_____ 22. Adult students often lack necessary study skills.

_____ 23. Maximum auditory acuity is attained by about fifteen years of age.

Exhibit 1. *(continued)*

_____ 24. The inability to hear can produce emotional disturbances such as depression, anxiety, and frustration.

_____ 25. Visual acuity attains its maximum at about eighteen years of age.

_____ 26. For normal learning tasks an adult of age thirty requires 120 watts of illumination, whereas by age fifty, 180 watts are required.

_____ 27. With advancing age the lens loses its elasticity and cannot focus readily.

_____ 28. In the aging process there is a loss of auditory acuity on the high tones.

_____ 29. Speed of reaction time tends to decline with age.

_____ 30. As we age, we slow in our reaction to auditory stimuli.

_____ 31. A major change in distance acuity occurs between ages fifty and sixty.

_____ 32. Physical strength peaks between ages twenty-five and thirty.

_____ 33. Learning performance declines with age.

_____ 34. Frequently the fear of aging is more harmful than the aging process itself.

_____ 35. Adults, even more than children, are sensitive to failure in their learning situation.

_____ 36. Most adults enter a learning situation with a high readiness to learn.

_____ 37. Adults rarely hold the opinion that they are unable to learn.

_____ 38. Once the adult has formed a perception of a stimulus, it is difficult to change that perception.

_____ 39. The concept of developmental tasks provides a way of identifying the educational needs of adults.

_____ 40. Emotional association with words or events does not affect the adult in gaining new knowledge.

_____ 41. A phenomenon of the adult years is the universal experience that time seems to pass more quickly as one ages.

_____ 42. Adulthood is not a developmental period in itself.

_____ 43. The adult has a less realistic attitude toward time than youth.

_____ 44. In the adult learning process, external motivation is usually more effective than internal motivation.

The facilitator distributes the questionnaire and asks each individual to complete it. This should take about ten to fifteen minutes. The facilitator then divides the large group into at least four subgroups of three to six participants. The first subgroup is instructed to discuss items 1 to 11; the second subgroup, items 12 to 22; the third subgroup, items 23 to 33; and the fourth subgroup, items 34 to 44. This discussion has two main purposes: (1) to allow participants to interact with the information (for example, to share insights and knowledge, reflect on the information as it relates to the adult experience, and ask for clarification) and (2) to determine consensus regarding the correct answer for each question. (Consensus in this case means substantive agreement, not necessarily a majority decision as determined by voting.) If participants cannot arrive at consensus for any item, a group recorder should mark that item to report back to the larger group. The subgroup discussion phase usually takes thirty to forty-five minutes.

The facilitator reconvenes the group and discusses questionnaire items 1 to 11, emphasizing those items for which consensus was not reached by the respective subgroup. The same process is undertaken for items 12 to 22, 23 to 33, and 34 to 44. The facilitator's familiarity with the source summaries (Exhibit 2) in this chapter as well as additional information in Chapters One and Eight of this sourcebook is essential to successful group discussion. Discussion may take thirty to ninety minutes, depending on depth, interest, and available time.

For situations involving large groups, the facilitator should divide the participants into subgroups of five to six persons. The subgroups should be labeled A, B, C, and D. All the A groups would discuss items 1 to 11, the B groups would discuss items 12 to 22, the C groups would discuss items 23 to 33, and the D groups would discuss items 34 to 44. A variation of this process would be for each subgroup to discuss and reach consensus on all items.

Implications of the RALI

Technique. The awareness of adult development principles generated by the administration and discussion of the RALI has helped teachers, counselors, and adult learners adapt their teaching, counseling, and learning styles to be more consistent with adult development theory. A technique found to be helpful to various groups in translating theory into practice follows.

The facilitator divides the larger group into four subgroups (A, B, C, and D) of three to six participants to discuss implications of the RALI to their personal and professional interests. Subgroup A is asked to develop a list of at least five specific implications either to themselves as learners or to their professions based on RALI items 1 to 11 (orientation to learning). Subgroup B is asked to develop a similar list of at least five specific implications based on RALI items 12 to 22 (mental abilities). Subgroup C is given the same task based on RALI items 23 to 33 (physiological factors), and subgroup D is asked to develop a list based on RALI items 34 to 44 (psychological factors). In this manner the four categories of the RALI are used.

Outcomes for the Adult Educator. The implication technique generates much practical information for use by educators, counselors, and adult learners. For example, with regard to discussion of the *orientation group,* the adult educator can

1. Involve the learners in establishing measurable objectives based on perceived needs
2. Provide educational experiences based on job and/or life situations
3. Allow adults to set their own learning pace
4. Use the adult experience as a resource for learning
5. Integrate theory with practice
6. Provide the learners with continuous evaluation and feedback relating to their learning objectives

7. Use a problem-centered rather than a subject-centered approach to learning
8. Provide opportunities for adults to apply classroom instruction through use of simulation, case studies, and role playing
9. Use learning contracts
10. Provide opportunities for assessment of student needs.

Regarding discussion of the *mental abilities group*, the adult educator can do the following:

1. Stress the need for task accomplishment rather than speed
2. Build on the adult's strength in areas of stored knowledge and vocabulary
3. Relate new or difficult concepts to the existing experiential base
4. Provide necessary study skills
5. Eliminate unnecessary anxieties such as timed tests and emphasizing mistakes
6. Involve learners in self-diagnosis of competencies and learning styles
7. Employ a variety of teaching styles.

With regard to discussion of the *physiological factors group*, the adult educator can

1. Ensure that lighting is adequate and without glare
2. Prepare instructional material using maximum contrast
3. Use strong rather than subtle tints when using color
4. Leave written material on board as long as possible, as adult learners require more time to copy such material
5. Speak slowly and distinctly and with sufficient volume
6. Use short rather than overly long sentences
7. Arrange the learning environment in such a way that the learners can see each other's faces
8. Eliminate background noise when possible
9. Provide comfortable seats and a comfortable temperature setting.

Finally, in relation to the discussion of the *psychological factors group*, the adult educator can

1. Create a supportive, threat-free, and accepting learning environment
2. Arrange opportunities for learners to interact in groups
3. Avoid "busy work"
4. Base instruction on developmental tasks
5. Eliminate unnecessary time requirements
6. Stress intrinsic rather than extrinsic motivation
7. Capitalize on the adult's experience
8. Demonstrate belief in the adult's capability to learn
9. Consider pass/no-credit options for initial courses

10. Provide positive reinforcement for accomplishments
11. Create opportunities for adults to engage in reflective thinking and writing
12. Use formative evaluation to communicate progress
13. Treat adults with respect.

Outcomes for Counselors and Advisers. Implications for counselors (or advisers) include the following:

1. Work with adults to attain a more realistic awareness of the aging process
2. Compensate for the verbal-quantitative discrepancy by initially channeling the adult into courses in the humanities and social sciences and away from science and math
3. Suggest refresher courses in math
4. Advise returning students to take practical courses dealing with reading comprehension, writing, and study skills and academic survival when necessary
5. Establish specific and attainable goals and objectives
6. Explore related fields or areas where skills can be updated with minimum retraining
7. Minimize exploratory activity by providing current information
8. Minimize time requirements by using existing testing services such as College-Level Examination Program (CLEP), Defense Activity for Non-Traditional Educational Support (DANTES), and American College Testing Program/Proficiency Examination Program (ACT/PEP)
9. Assist in developing assessment of prior learning portfolios
10. Provide information on nontraditional adult education opportunities
11. Compensate for the adult's frequent lack of confidence in his or her learning abilities by beginning academic programs with a minimum rather than a maximum course load
12. Expedite the multirole status of adults by providing flexibility in course selection and programming, establishing goals that do not bankrupt the family emotionally, and providing emotional support for the learner
13. Help the adult to establish short-term as well as long-term goals and objectives
14. Serve as a resource for the faculty to help establish the most productive learning environment.

Outcomes for Adult Learners. Implications for adult learners include the following:

1. Locate an educational institution that stresses integration, interpretation, and application rather than mere acquisition of information
2. Record lectures to listen to and learn from independently

3. Explore alternative delivery systems that allow for self-paced learning (for example, correspondence courses, independent studies, television courses, computer-based learning tapes, newspaper courses)
4. Utilize previous learning by becoming knowledgeable about options such as credit by standardized exams (for example, CLEP, DANTES, ACT/PEP), previously evaluated programs including American Council on Education (ACE) guides, licenses, certificates, portfolio assessment, advanced placement exams, and challenge exams
5. Be cognizant of organizations such as the Council for Adult and Experiential Learning (CAEL) that can assist in obtaining information about assessment of prior learning and education resources in your region of the country
6. Become an "informed consumer" by critically investigating all possible educational opportunities—nontraditional adult-oriented programs as well as traditional programs
7. Learn about and understand individual learning styles
8. Trust instincts and do not put undue emphasis on "outside experts"
9. Request ongoing feedback on educational performance
10. Have a complete physical examination, with special emphasis on vision and hearing, prior to beginning an educational program.

Conclusion

The use of the RALI allows faculty and adult learners to determine the extent to which they are aware of adult learner characteristics and to understand the implications these characteristics have for both teaching and learning. This understanding allows faculty and learners to engage in purposeful development and growth. As Daloz (1986) states, "We *need* to teach. . . . We teach not just for our students but for ourselves as well. . . . Without the affirmation born of extending ourselves beyond self-preservation, . . . the questions that might enable us to move on toward something like wisdom would go unasked. We need our students as much as they need us" (pp. 242–243).

Exhibit 2. RALI Answers and Source Summary

The following section includes questionnaire answers and a source summary for the four factors of the RALI: (1) orientation to learning, (2) mental abilities, (3) physiological factors, and (4) psychological factors.

Orientation to Learning

1. *True.* An adult brings to learning situations a tremendous range of stored learning—the accumulation of experiences in everyday living. These are useful resources for learning (Lorge, 1963; Ausubel, 1968; Hendrickson, 1970; Brundage and Mackeracher, 1980).

Exhibit 2. *(continued)*

2. *True.* The adult's time perspective changes from one of postponed application of knowledge to immediacy of application. Accordingly, the orientation to learning shifts from being subject centered to being problem centered (Comfort, 1974; Knowles, 1984). Research generally supports the notion that most adults who voluntarily undertake a learning project do so more in the hope of solving a problem than with the intention of learning a subject (Knowles, 1980; Cross, 1981).

3. *True.* The more experience a person has had, the more the past probably will interfere with the present. It is easier for an experienced person to learn a completely new task than to do a familiar task in a new way (Zahn, 1967; Smith, 1982).

4. *True.* The more the facilitator of learning can relate information to the experience of the learner, the better and faster the adult will learn. Thus, the adult learner should be encouraged to integrate new or difficult concepts with personal experiences and to use this experience to help with the present and the future (Whipple, 1957; Zahn, 1967). Cross (1981) concludes that most adults are responding to transitions in which needs for new job skills or for knowledge pertaining to family life serve as "triggers" and imitate learning activity. As a rule, adults like their learning activities to be meaningful to their life situations, and they want the learning outcomes to have some immediacy of application (Tough, 1979; Knowles, 1984; Brookfield, 1986).

5. *True.* Tough (1979), Aslanian and Brickell (1980), and Knowles (1984) indicate that adults are constantly engaged in learning, and only a relatively small percentage of their learning occurs in a classroom.

6. *True.* For many adults, especially older and more experienced ones, long experience will cause them to be set in their ways and resentful of change (Zahn, 1967; Hendrickson, 1970; Kidd, 1973). The adult's reservoir of past experience represents both a potentially rich resource for learning and an obstacle to learning (Smith, 1982).

7. *False.* Adults are inclined to distribute their energy and involvement according to the kind and amounts of learning perceived to be most beneficial immediately and for the future. Adults should be able to influence their own learning goals as a means of ensuring that their goals meet their specific needs (Jensen, 1963; Comfort, 1974). One unequivocal implication of adults' different orientations toward life and of their broader experience bases is that they can usually identify or help to identify what they need to learn (Smith, 1982).

8. *True.* Many adults desire minimum time expenditure to complete educational objectives, as they have compelling responsibilities that compete for time and attention (Comfort, 1974). In most surveys, lack of time rivals cost for first place among the obstacles to education (Cross, 1981).

9. *False.* Many adult facilitators are not provided with appropriate information about the biological, psychological, and sociological aspects of adult development and have made the erroneous assumption that adults and children have the same orientation to learning (Birren and Woodruff, 1973). Adults enter into education with a different time perspective from that of children, which in turn produces a difference in the way adults view learning (Knowles, 1980).

10. *False.* According to Knowles (1984) and Chickering (1981), as individuals grow older, they tend to demonstrate an ever-increasing range of individual differences.

Exhibit 2. *(continued)*

11. *False.* Older students are able to learn most effectively when they set their own pace, when they take periodic breaks, and when learning episodes are distributed according to a rationale dictated by content (Knox, 1977; Brundage and Mackeracher, 1980).

Mental Abilities

12. *False.* Botwinick (1973) reports that the classical pattern of verbal and performance scores changing with age has been replicated many times and now constitutes one of the best-replicated results in the literature. Cattell (1963) makes a distinction between fluid and crystallized intelligence, contending that the two types of intelligence show different patterns in aging that are complementary in terms of adaptation. Baltes, Dittman-Kohli, and Dixon (1984) emphasize a distinction between the mechanics and the pragmatics of intelligence.

13. *True.* Sharon (1971) indicates that the pattern of the scores in different disciplines changes as a function of age. Performance on tests of humanities, social science, and history improves with age, while achievement in mathematics and the natural sciences declines. Knox (1986) notes that performance in learner tasks such as vocabulary and general information improves during adulthood.

14. *True.* The early work by Thorndike, Bregman, Tilton, and Woodyard (1928) established this basic premise. After age forty, increasing psychomotor slowness is often an important factor in explaining individual performance (Long, 1983).

15. *True.* Thorndike, Bregman, Tilton, and Woodyard (1928) established that age clearly impacts the time required to complete a task. The only thing that decreases with age is the rate of learning, not the ability to learn. In general it can be concluded that the time required for learning new things increases with age (Cross, 1981). Salthouse (1985) and Poon (1987) indicate that older adults tend to be slower and have more problems learning new information.

16. *True.* One of the most significant problems in assessing an adult's ability is the degree to which information has been obtained from cross-sectional rather than longitudinal studies. The decline in intellectual function with increasing age intimated by cross-sectional data (Jones and Conrad, 1933; Wechsler, 1955) has not been supported by longitudinal studies, which indicate growth into middle age and beyond. When a wide range of learning abilities is included, the general conclusion is that most adults in their forties and fifties have about the same ability to learn as they had in their twenties and thirties, particularly when they can control the pace (Knox, 1977).

17. *True.* Darkenwald and Merriam (1982) surmise that adults' readiness to learn depends on the amount of their previous learning.

18. *False.* Bilash and Zubek (1960), Owens (1966), and others have provided reliable data reporting that scores in perceptual and dexterity tests declined from the teen years through the seventies. Manual dexterity is greatest at about age thirty-three; then the hands and fingers become progressively more clumsy (Schlossberg, 1978).

19. *False.* Bischof (1969) has reported that adult performance in intelligence tests calls for certain attributes such as being motivated and persisting in the task in order for the adult to perform well.

20. *True.* Early studies by Knox and Sjogren (1965) and Sjogren, Knox, and Grotelueschen (1968) consistently found that not only level of education but also

Exhibit 2. *(continued)*

recency of participation in the educational activity were related to an adult's ability to learn. Knox (1977) found recency of participation in formal education to be correlated with more effective learning.

21. *False.* Kolb (1981), Smith (1982), and Knox (1986) contend that adults accumulate many life experiences, resulting in a distinct preference for modes of learning and thereby resulting in individual learning styles.

22. *True.* According to Larson (1970), too few teachers know enough about the adult learner's anxiety level. Many adult students feel they do not possess the necessary study skills (Comfort, 1974).

Physiological Factors

23. *True.* In most people the peak of auditory performance seems to be reached before the fifteenth birthday, and there is a gradual but consistent decline until about age sixty-five (Kidd, 1973; Florida Department of Education, 1973; Kimmel, 1974).

24. *True.* The inability to hear can produce emotional disturbances such as fear, insecurity, and the inability to learn new concepts (Florida Department of Education, 1973). The psychological damage may be more serious than the actual physical impairment (Cross, 1981). Woodruff-Pak (1988) indicates that hearing loss can impair an individual's capacity for interaction as it interferes with the ability to understand communication.

25. *True.* Visual acuity increases during childhood and early adolescence and then remains quite stable between twenty and forty years of age (Knox, 1977). In most circumstances, peak visual functioning occurs during late adolescence or early adulthood (Hayslip and Panek, 1989).

26. *True.* For normal learning tasks after age fifty, the amount of illumination becomes a critical factor. A fifty-year-old is likely to need 50 percent more illumination than a twenty-year-old (Cross, 1981).

27. *True.* With increasing age, there is a decrease in the ability of the eye to focus on objects at varying distances. This results mainly from a loss of elasticity in the lens of the eye (Hayslip and Panek, 1989). Between the ages of twenty and fifty, there is typically an appreciable loss of accommodation power and elasticity of the lens, after which the decline is more gradual (Knox, 1977; Rogers, 1986).

28. *True.* Most individuals above the age of forty will probably show some loss of high-tone perception (Botwinick, 1973; Rogers, 1986; Brant, Wood, and Fozard, 1986).

29. *True.* One effect of aging (in the absence of disease) is a slowing of reaction time, regardless of the sensory modality and regardless of the muscle used for the response (Kimmel, 1974; Woodruff-Pak, 1988). After age forty, increasing psychomotor slowness is often an important factor in explaining individual differences (Long, 1983).

30. *True.* Throughout the adult lifetime there is a slowing of the central auditory processes to auditory stimuli. For this reason many aging individuals find it difficult to follow rapid speech in spite of little or no hearing loss (Hand, 1973; Woodruff-Pak, 1988).

31. *False.* For the general population vision is at its best at about age eighteen; it then declines gradually until around age forty, at which time there is a sharp decline for the next fifteen years (Cross, 1981). Uncorrected distance acuity declines rapidly between ages forty and sixty (Fozard, Gittings, and Schock, 1986).

Exhibit 2. *(continued)*

32. *True.* Strength peaks between ages twenty-five and thirty, after which the muscles—particularly in the back and legs—weaken unless maintained by exercise (Schlossberg, 1978; Hodgson and Busherk, 1981; Rogers, 1986).

33. *False.* It is now generally agreed that if there is an age limit on learning performance, it is not likely to occur until around age seventy-five (Kidd, 1973).

Psychological Factors

34. *True.* The elderly frequently appear to live in a social climate that is not conducive to feelings of adequacy, usefulness, security, and good adjustment in later years. If these concepts are subsumed by the adult learner, the fear of aging, rather than the aging process itself, may induce mental deterioration (Horvath and Horvath, 1952). While physical functioning may decline gradually, physical appearance may deteriorate at a rate that can make one feel older (Biehler and Hudson, 1986).

35. *True.* Warren (1961) contends that adults are even more sensitive than children to failure in their learning situations and that previous unfavorable experiences with education may cause fears and self-doubts about ability (Comfort, 1974).

36. *True.* In general adults come to the learning situation with a high readiness to learn, but they need answers that relate directly to their lives (Axford, 1980).

37. *False.* Many adults still harbor doubts about their personal learning ability. For adults to undertake a return to school or an in-depth learning project is for them to move into unknown territory, regardless of their educational level and personal resources (Smith, 1982).

38. *True.* The way adults organize their perceptions and what they select to perceive are influenced by expectations. It is more difficult to change the perceptions of an adult than those of a child, as the adult has had more experience than a child (Zahn, 1967; Whitbourne, 1986).

39. *True.* The tasks an individual must learn—the developmental tasks of life—are those things that constitute healthy and satisfactory growth in our society. They are excellent starting points to identify educational needs of adults (Cross, 1981; Whitbourne, 1986). Brundage and Mackeracher (1980) indicate that adults are strongly motivated to learn in areas relevant to their current developmental tasks, social roles, life crises, and transition periods.

40. *False.* Adults actually have more emotional associations with factual material than do children. The devices of control are more elaborate and better covered in the adult (Murphy, 1955). Whitbourne (1986) has indicated that emotions and attitudes influence the ways in which individuals learn new information.

41. *True.* Most would agree that as one ages, time seems to pass more quickly. For a youngster of six, one year is one-sixth of a lifetime. For a youth of sixteen, a year is one-sixteenth of life. For a man of forty, a year is one-fortieth of his life, and at seventy merely one-seventieth of the years lived (McClusky, 1963).

42. *False.* As Havighurst (1972) points out, life consists of many developmental periods. Smith (1982) has observed that adults pass through a number of developmental phases in the physical, psychological, and social spheres.

43. *False.* Lewin says that to the child the future is "vague but just ahead, to the adolescent vague but unlimited; the adult, however, has a realistic attitude toward time which sharply differentiates his or her perspective from the outlook of youth" (McClusky, 1963, p. 18). Neugarten (1963) and Long (1983) believe that there comes a point, usually in the middle years, when the individual realizes

Exhibit 2. *(continued)*

that time is not infinite and that the self will die. Along with this realization may come an end to measuring one's lifetime from the date of one's birth, and, instead, a beginning to measuring it by the distance to one's death.

44. *False.* There are many different notions about motivation and its influence on learning. Most would agree that intrinsic motivation is far more important than extrinsic motivation, especially when dealing with adult learners in noncredit situations (Verner and Davison, 1971; Wlodkowski, 1984). Darkenwald and Merriam (1982) surmise that intrinsic motivation produces more persuasive and permanent learning.

References

Aslanian, C. B., and Brickell, H. M. *Americans in Transition.* New York: College Entrance Examination Board, 1980.

Ausubel, D. P. *Educational Psychology: A Cognitive View.* New York: Holt, Rinehart & Winston, 1968.

Axford, R. W. *Adult Education: The Open Door to Lifelong Learning.* Indiana, Pa.: A. G. Halldin, 1980.

Baltes, P. B., Dittman-Kohli, F., and Dixon, R. "New Perspectives on the Development of Intelligence in Adulthood: Toward a Dual Process Conception and a Model of Selective Optimization with Compensation." In P. Baltes and O. Brim (eds.), *Life-Span Development and Behavior.* Vol. 6. New York: Academic Press, 1984.

Biehler, R. F., and Hudson, L. M. *Developmental Psychology: An Introduction.* Boston: Houghton Mifflin, 1986.

Bilash, I., and Zubek, J. D. "The Effects of Age on Factorially 'Pure' Mental Abilities." *Journal of Gerontology,* 1960, *15,* 175–182.

Birren, J. E. *The Psychology of Aging.* Englewood Cliffs, N.J.: Prentice-Hall, 1964.

Birren, J. E., and Woodruff, D. S. "A Life-Span Perspective for Education." *New York University Education Quarterly,* 1973, pp. 25–31.

Bischof, L. J. *Adult Psychology.* New York: Harper & Row, 1969.

Botwinick, J. *Aging and Behavior.* New York: Springer, 1973.

Brant, L. J., Wood, J. L., and Fozard, J. L. "Age Changes in Hearing Thresholds." *Gerontologist,* 1986, *26,* 156.

Brookfield, S. D. *Understanding and Facilitating Adult Learning: A Comprehensive Analysis of Principles and Effective Practices.* San Francisco: Jossey-Bass, 1986.

Brundage, D. H., and Mackeracher, D. *Adult Learning Principles and Their Application to Program Planning.* Toronto: Toronto Ministry of Education, 1980.

Cattell, R. B. "Theory of Fluid and Crystallized Intelligence: A Critical Experiment." *Journal of Educational Psychology,* 1963, *54* (1), 1–22.

Chickering, A. W., and Associates (eds.). *The Modern American College: Responding to the New Realities of Diverse Students and a Changing Society.* San Francisco: Jossey-Bass, 1981.

Comfort, R. W. "Higher Adult Education Program: A Model." *Adult Leadership,* May 1974, pp. 6–8, 25–29, 32.

Cross, K. P. *Adults as Learners: Increasing Participation and Facilitating Learning.* San Francisco: Jossey-Bass, 1981.

Daloz, L. A. *Effective Teaching and Mentoring: Realizing the Transformational*

Power of Adult Learning Experiences. San Francisco: Jossey-Bass, 1986.

Darkenwald, G. G., and Merriam, S. B. *Adult Education: Foundations of Practice.* New York: Harper & Row, 1982.

Florida Department of Education. *A Review of Physiological and Psychological Changes in Aging and Their Implications for Teachers of Adults.* Tallahassee, Fla.: Department of Education, July 1973.

Fozard, J. L., Gittings, N. S., and Schock, N. W. "Age Changes in Visual Acuity." *Gerontologist,* 1986, *26,* 158.

Hand, S. E. "What It Means to Teach Older Adults." In A. Hendrickson (ed.), *A Manual on Planning Educational Programs for Older Adults.* Tallahassee: Department of Adult Education, Florida State University, 1973.

Havighurst, R. J. *Developmental Tasks and Education.* New York: McKay, 1972.

Hayslip, B., Jr., and Panek, P. E. *Adult Development and Aging.* New York: Harper & Row, 1989.

Hendrickson, A. "Teaching Adult Illiterates." In V. J. Amana (ed.), *Heuristics of Adult Education.* Boulder: University of Colorado, 1970.

Hodgson, J. L., and Busherk, E. R. "The Role of Exercise in Aging." In P. Danon, N. W. Schoeh, and M. Marais (eds.), *Aging: A Challenge to Science and Society.* Vol. 1. London: Oxford University Press, 1981.

Horvath, E. C., and Horvath, S. M. "Physical and Mental Health in the Aged." *Journal of the Iowa Medical Society* (Des Moines), 1952, *42,* 47-51.

Jensen, G. "Socio-Psychological Foundations of Adult Learning." In I. Lorge, H. Y. McClusky, G. Jensen, and W. C. Hallenbeck (eds.), *Psychology of Adults.* Washington, D.C.: Adult Education Association of the U.S.A., 1963.

Jones, H. E., and Conrad, H. S. "The Growth and Decline of Intelligence." *General Psychological Monograph,* 1933, *13,* 223-298.

Kidd, J. R. *How Adults Learn.* New York: Association Press, 1973.

Kimmel, D. C. *Adulthood and Aging.* New York: Wiley, 1974.

Knowles, M. S. *The Modern Practice of Adult Education: From Pedagogy to Andragogy.* (2nd. ed.) New York: Cambridge Books, 1980.

Knowles, M. S. *The Adult Learner: A Neglected Species.* (3rd ed.) Houston, Tex.: Gulf, 1984.

Knox, A. B. *Adult Development and Learning: A Handbook on Individual Growth and Competence in the Adult Years.* San Francisco: Jossey-Bass, 1977.

Knox, A. B. *Helping Adults Learn: A Guide to Planning, Implementing, and Conducting Programs.* San Francisco: Jossey-Bass, 1986.

Knox, A. B., and Sjogren, D. "Research on Adult Learning." *Adult Education,* 1965, *15,* 133-137.

Kolb, D. A. "Learning Styles and Disciplinary Differences." In A. W. Chickering and Associates (eds.), *The Modern American College: Responding to the New Realities of Diverse Students and a Changing Society.* San Francisco: Jossey-Bass, 1981.

Larson, C. G. "The Adult Learner: A Review of Recent Research." *Vocational Journal,* September 1970, pp. 67-68.

Long, H. B. *Adult Learning: Research and Practice.* New York: Cambridge University Press, 1983.

Lorge, I. "The Adult Learner." In I. Lorge, H. Y. McClusky, G. Jensen, and W. C. Hallenbeck (eds.), *Psychology of Adults.* Washington, D.C.: Adult Education Association of the U.S.A., 1963.

McClusky, H. Y. "The Course of the Adult Life Span." In I. Lorge, H. Y. McClusky, G. Jensen, and W. C. Hallenbeck (eds.), *Psychology of Adults.* Washington, D.C.: Adult Education Association of the U.S.A., 1963.

Murphy, G. *Psychological Needs of Adults: A Symposium by Gardner Murphy and Raymond Kuhlen.* Chicago: Center for the Study of Liberal Education for Adults, 1955.

Neugarten, B. L. "Personality Changes During the Adult Years." In R. G. Kuhlen (ed.), *Psychological Backgrounds of Adult Education.* Chicago: Center for the Study of Liberal Education for Adults, 1963.

Owens, W. A., Jr. "Age and Mental Abilities: A Second Adult Follow-Up." *Journal of Educational Psychology*, 1966, pp. 311-325.

Poon, L. W. "Learning." In G. H. Maddox and others (eds.), *Encyclopedia of Aging.* New York: Springer, 1987.

Rogers, D. *The Adult Years.* Englewood Cliffs, N.J.: Prentice-Hall, 1986.

Rossman, M. E. "Awareness of Adult Characteristics by the Faculty in the Maricopa County Community College District." Unpublished doctoral dissertation, University of Massachusetts, 1977.

Salthouse, T. A. "Speed of Behavior and Its Implications for Cognition." In J. E. Birren and K. W. Schaie (eds.), *Handbook of the Psychology of Aging.* (2nd. ed.) New York: Van Nostrand Reinhold, 1985.

Schlossberg, N. K. *Perspectives on Counseling Adults: Issues and Skills.* Malabar, Fla.: Kreiger, 1978.

Sharon, A. T. "Adult Academic Achievement in Relation to Formal Education and Age." *Adult Education*, 1971, *21* (4), 231-237.

Sjogren, D., Knox, A. B., and Grotelueschen, A. "Adult Learning in Relation to Prior Adult Education Participation." *Adult Education Journal*, 1968, *19* (1), 3-10.

Smith, R. M. *Learning How to Learn.* Chicago: Follett, 1982.

Thorndike, R. L., Bregman, E. O., Tilton, W. J., and Woodyard, E. *Adult Learning.* New York: Macmillan, 1928.

Tough, A. *The Adult's Learning Projects: A Fresh Approach to Theory and Practice in Adult Learning.* Toronto: Ontario Institute for Studies in Education, 1979.

Verner, C., and Davison, C. *Psychological Factors in Adult Learning and Education.* Tallahassee: Florida State University, 1971.

Warren, V. B. *How Adults Can Learn More—Faster.* Washington, D.C.: National Association of Public School Adult Educators, 1961.

Wechsler, D. *The Measurement of Adult Intelligence.* (Rev. ed.) Baltimore, Md.: Williams & Wilkins, 1955.

Whipple, J. B. *Especially for Adults.* Boston: Center for the Study of Liberal Education for Adults, 1957.

Whitbourne, S. K. *Adult Development.* New York: Praeger, 1986.

Wlodkowski, R. J. *Enhancing Adult Motivation to Learn: A Guide to Improving Instruction and Increasing Learner Achievement.* San Francisco: Jossey-Bass, 1985.

Woodruff-Pak, D. S. *Psychology and Aging.* Englewood Cliffs, N.J.: Prentice-Hall, 1988.

Zahn, J. C. "Differences Between Adults and Youth Affecting Learning." *Adult Education*, 1967, *17* (2), 67-77.

Maxine E. Rossman is professor of education and psychology at Ottawa University, Phoenix Center.

Mark H. Rossman is professor of education and director of graduate studies at Ottawa University, Phoenix Center.

The author presents his pioneering work using psychodrama with adult learners.

Psychodrama: Discovering New Meaning in Personal Drama

William D. Pearlman

> Man lives in the meanings he is able to discern.
>
> —Michael Polyani and Harry Prosch

For those of us who came of age when liberal arts studies were the usual course, there was the constant sense that education and the meaning of existence were inextricably linked. In my work in adult education, I have been developing ideas and classroom techniques that borrow from several fields—theater studies, analytical psychology, film studies, actors' training—all of which have led me in the direction of using psychodrama as the basis for an educational process that aims at heightened states of meaning and utilizes many concepts of adult development. The basis of this exploration comes from the sense that psychodrama can create a unique kind of living coherence and meaningful home in the context of classroom work. And the matrix of the work is the adult's own personal development, in all its diversity and complexity. In what follows I explore the nature of psychodrama and its unique capacity to serve as an educational instrument. I start with a short history of its development and proceed to an examination of its relationship to depth psychology, dramatic imagination, and the whole realm of beneficial aspects associated with significant play.

Classic psychodrama was first developed by Jacob Moreno, a Viennese psychiatrist who created a "theater of truth" in his early work and later developed the first psychodrama institute in the United States. Psychodrama has become one of the "action therapies" and is used all over the world in a variety of settings and with many different populations.

Application

For several years, I have been investigating a form of psychodrama that is both a therapeutic exercise and a pedagogical format for understanding the dynamics of emotional and cognitive development. The work feels so promising perhaps because it proceeds from inside the individual "actor" whose imaginative powers are tested on this unique and personal stage.

The conceptual components in Moreno's psychodrama system are divided into five major categories: spontaneity, situation, tele, catharsis, and insight. Spontaneity, for Moreno, is an improvised and adequate response to a new situation or a new and adequate response to an old situation. Situation is a place where everything occurs in the here and now, and barriers of time and distance are transcended. Moreno uses the Greek prefix *tele* to convey the ability to fully empathize with another's experience, "eye to eye and face to face." Catharsis, discussed later, is used by Moreno in the Aristotelian sense of the purging of fear and pity that occurs when experiencing a tragic hero's fall. Insight refers to an increase in cognitive awareness or a broadening of the field of psychological knowledge through the psychodramatic experience.

Psychodrama stretches the adult's imagination in truly self-revelatory ways. It opens up a hidden landscape of unconscious problems and issues that can lead to serious reflection and change. In a typical psychodrama, a person focuses on something that matters very deeply. It starts with a warm-up, a free association concerned with how the person is in the world, what is going on, what is bothering her or him. It might begin by talking about marriage, the family, the job, or hopes for the future. The individual might not be ready for a large enactment but might choose instead to stay in a circumscribed reality; we might simply ask the participant to improvise a monologue or speak to an invisible "other" in an empty chair. The group is charged with being respectful of a person's rights and privacy. Within the group there are four categories or activities: the protagonist, the helper, the observer, and the director. The helper functions as auxiliary ego or double, entering into important roles in the protagonist's enactment. The observer watches the drama and enters into the sharing at the drama's end. Observers are asked to share personal experience, not to analyze or give advice. The director guides the dramatic movement, testing the emotional heat of the protagonist, preparing auxiliaries, and stopping the action when necessary.

The world of the psychodrama is the world of shared meaning. It starts with a simple group interaction. The director wonders how everyone is doing. Where do we want to go today? Whose issues are paramount in terms of the group's needs? Moreno was interested in sociometric guides that discover what the whole group is doing emotionally. This spontaneous, broad interplay between the group and the individual makes possible a heartfelt investigation of the nature of the modern world (as seen in this particular microcosm).

Smith and Berg (1987) put this interplay in another context: "The key issue is how members and the group as a whole find a voice to give expression to what is going on. By focusing on explicit behaviors, patterns that develop iconic meaning for group members, and what is left unsaid along with what is expressed, the many ways voices develop in a group can be examined. Acting while remaining silent and being visible while remaining hidden are both ways of speaking in a group, and each mode may be giving expression to important facets of group life" (p. 131). And again, "There is a precariousness to self-discovery that is like living on the edge, swinging between the tensions of what is and what might be" (p. 147).

This is true of all groups, but it is even more deeply true of the psychodramatic group. To find oneself seriously engaged in a group dynamic requires the courage to discover something new about oneself in the group context. The individual may regress, may feel overwhelmed by the group's authority and power, or may feel at risk in a whole array of psychological ways. The group becomes an occasion that demands a kind of faith. Self-disclosure becomes a movement beyond deep and painful doubts, and the activity of the group encourages the descent, even gives it a new life. Again and again we find in the psychodramatic theater (in which the self struggles with huge inner and outer forces) the need to overcome obstacles to self-affirmation. The group provides a stage on which this most important action can find speech and gesture.

The director in the psychodrama session is usually the adult educator and is both mentor and theorist. There is a constant movement back and forth between the action of a particular psychodrama and the material that it generates. The psychodrama loosely follows principles derived from psychoanalysis and psychological aspects of adult development. There is a kind of regression that allows early group (family) experience to be reworked. It requires an embracing of complexes and regressive tendencies fully supported by the group, which provides a kind of transferential basis for the work. Unconscious intrapsychic material is activated when other group members assume roles in the psychodrama. In such a case we can talk of the movement of inner "stuff" onto the stage, where there can be a fresh exploration of emotional ground. There is also in the work the sense that the participants—particularly the protagonist—can spontaneously explore what is in fact a repeated pattern (with, say, a relative) in a new way. And this is a new experience, born of the imaginative paradox that is psychodrama's insistent new wine in old bottles.

The drama enacted in the personal theater of the protagonist requires some kind of attempt at speech that gets to the heart of the issues being considered. At its best it requires a reaching after words of substance, "soul-speech," echoing James Hillman (1975), who says, "A mark of imaginal man is the speech of his soul, and the range of this speech, its self-generative spontaneity, its precise subtlety and ambiguous suggestion, its capacity, as Hegel said, 'to receive and reproduce every modification of our ideational faculty,' can be supplanted neither by the technology of communication media, by contemplative spiritual silence, nor by physical gestures and signs" (p. 275). The call to come forth and be heard, to speak from our soul's deepest center, is certainly part of what is required in the dramatic events in which our protagonists find themselves. Can they do it? It depends on their passion for meaning. It depends on their ability to open up to something that is both personal and archetypal. The dramas enacted bear the potential for dealing not only with the personal tribulations that occur in relation to mothers, daughters, or husbands but also with those parts of the personality that Jung referred to as shadow, self, ego, and anima, the various inner figures of the unconscious.

Archetypal Drama

In my work with adult students using psychodramatic methods, I have come to explore what I now call "archetypal drama," which is devoted primarily to dealing with problems and issues concerned with the archetypes. An operational way of reflecting on archetypes would be to think of them as root ideas, myth figures, dominant fantasies, or potentials of structure. From Hillman (1975) again, "But one thing is absolutely essential to the notion of archetypes: their emotional possessive effect, their bedazzlement of consciousness" (p. xiii).

The archetypal dramas that I have witnessed in workshops affirm for me that there is a dimension of our emotional makeup that lends itself to this reaching beyond the personal. The work takes on (in this archetypal mode) an almost dreamlike intensity. There is a probing for ways of relating and new ways of naming objectives. It can feel like groping for light in a dark cave, or it can suddenly feel as though we are dealing with numinous or sacred ideas. The director (adult educator), who serves as mediator between the ego world and the archetypal, may ask the protagonist if a guide to go into this strange underworld is wanted. The protagonist may appoint an archetypal auxiliary ego to play this important role in the drama. What is somewhat amazing in this context is that persons may enter the landscape of the archetypal and, without dramatic training, know how to help the protagonist realize his or her deepest concerns. It is as if something in us instinctively knows this level of activity. Perhaps it is born of early childhood imaginings or the quixotic fumblings with imaginary friends so often part of our first meetings with inner figures, for psychic reality means being inside the basic fabric of fantasy. The archetypes "direct all fantasy activity into its appointed paths," says Jung (1954, p. 136).

The question might arise of what the essential difference between the classroom and the therapy room is. Admittedly, there is an overlap. Both education and therapy are concerned with the whole person. One of the advantages of the adult learner is that she or he usually brings into the classroom richer and deeper experiences than would be the case with eighteen-to-twenty-one-year-old students. The adult student over thirty years of age has had to struggle with the perplexities of life and carries a certain emotional weight into the educational process. They may have experienced marriages, children, deaths in the family, job crises, and the deepening tribulations of modern life. This makes the process of education a more potent occasion for personal growth than would have been the case when these students were younger. Perhaps one responsibility of adult educators is to provide adult students a proper arena for seeing their lives in a new and experientially fruitful light.

The classroom can truly become a protected place where significance and purposeful activity can flourish. In this way the process of learning is imbued with a special compensatory quality: All the fleeting activity of daily life is stopped for a time, and the psyche can meet some of its abundant inner content.

Individuation

Hidden within our context is the question of personal development that Jung called individuation. By individuation we mean the collected possibilities of a person, the entire sweep of inner and outer potential. But the emphasis in development for the Jungians is largely inner growth, that mysterious area of life that we come to know only through inner work.

What is inner work? It is nothing less than becoming aware of the conjunction possible between the conscious and the unconscious. It is a grappling with dreams, with fantasies, with parts of ourselves that want expression. We can look at the life of the individual as an assemblage of parts or a community of players, and we need to collect ourselves, or perhaps re-collect ourselves, and give a home to the various and often disparate parts. In a psychodrama we might use various parts of the stage so that the different personas of an individual can have their say. We might have a place for the office worker, for the mother, for the lover, for the artist, for the child. We are truly many, and the way to learn how to deal with our multiplicities is at hand. It requires that we trust that our vast complexities can be contained, that we can truly cope with who and what we are. The psychodramatic stage is a way of seeing this largess in a controlled way, which allows a kind of self-educative look at our fields of activity. The beauty of the process is that it is a guided study, a remarkable effort to sustain the size of one's life while being reassured that it is a shared condition. For it is often in isolation that the menacing fears of incapacity take their weird turns in us, breeding self-judgment and sometimes condemnation.

With psychodrama the group is there, acknowledging the difficulty of traversing so much personal ground. To watch a life unfold in the temporal microcosm of a personal psychodrama is to watch a person come to grips with a multitude of factors. There are others, always others: children and spouses and aunts and grandparents and, of course, friends; and ideas: aspirations for a career change, a project long delayed, a trip to a foreign land—all parts of the individual's puzzle, which exists in a context with pieces stretching before and after. One often gets the sense that dealing with all this in one brief period of time requires a Herculean strength, a fierce ability to go through it, to look at it: What is it doing to me? Why am I here? It requires great attention and great support. The group becomes a sort of home base, and the eyes of a new system of friendliness produce for us an atmosphere in which we can breathe deeply in our attempt to bring a fresh perspective into view. As Jung (1959, p. 256) says, "Judging from all previous experience, we do have a right to assume that the importance of the unconscious is about equal to that of consciousness. Undoubtedly there are conscious attitudes which are surpassed by the unconscious—attitudes so badly adapted to the individual as a whole that the unconscious attitude or constellation is a far better expression of his essential nature."

Dreams

Jung talks eloquently of the compensatory activity of dreams. He posits the dream material as having a valuable content, capable of correcting or giving new life to the conscious attitudes of a person. Likewise, I think the personal dramatic material that comes from psychodrama serves as a compensation for much that is unlived by individuals. A mother with whom one never spoke intimately or a child who has gone off into the world without saying good-bye can be brought into the protagonist's field of activity again, allowing an experience very closely resembling the actual unfolding that might have taken place. The theater has always had a close relationship with the dream, with its well-lit presentations of actors parading before an audience sitting in the dark. "We are such stuff as dreams are made of," wrote Shakespeare in the speech summarizing

Prospero's life of magic (*The Tempest IV.1*), paralleling Shakespeare's own explorations of magic in the theater. The figures of our dreams are not unlike the characters that embody complex psychic powers in plays. The theater, too, has a strangely compensatory quality in that it gives back a certain amount of freedom and meaning. Theater for the Greeks was the arena of Dionysus, about whom Michael Goldman (1975) writes, "Dionysus may be described as everything mysterious in the outside world that threatens to overwhelm the individual and every impulse in the individual that longs to be free of the limits the world imposes" (p. 14).

The psychodrama is a unique occasion for becoming the chief actor in one's own dramatic enterprise, and, with the help of others, to cast one's own play with living actors who will contribute to one's theatrical story. It can be an exhilarating business, trying out a spontaneous dramatic event in which the work is instigated and created by the person who decides to attempt such a personal production.

What is the potential outcome of a psychodramatic experience? Again, this parallels the theater. The object of Greek tragedy was catharsis, or a purging of fear and pity, a letting loose of suffering. The same thing often happens in a psychodrama: An emotional vigor is released, and there is a sense of reaching the center of one's inner life, of feeling absorbed in one's own dramatic intensity. The group may serve as a kind of sustaining force for the work, an audience whose attention keeps the work focused. Anxieties, fears, and other emotional or situational barriers may be faced directly through psychodrama. Drama and education meet in a charged arena wherein, as Martin Buber (1985) once wrote, "It is not the educational intention but . . . the meeting which is educationally fruitful." The sharing of deep emotional material and the group's persistent cohesion in the face of tremendous personal forces (for each protagonist) become a rallying of mutuality that can be tremendously invigorating.

Benefits

The actual learning that occurs in a psychodrama is as various as it would be in the classical theater. One person may have a spectacular breakthrough while the drama is being enacted; another may have the experience of profound insight days or weeks later. The thing to emphasize is that the dramatic event that occurs on the imaginative psychodrama stage is an experience that can touch the self in powerful ways—physically, emotionally, and spiritually. Just as one might be moved to run out of a theater after hearing the G-Minor Symphony by Mozart or seeing a great performance of *King Lear*, feeling cleansed and absorbed by the beauty, depth, and vigor of the work, so the same kind of sensation can accompany the adult learner returning to the world after a successful psychodramatic session.

And just as in great tragedy there is a recovery of truth only after tremendous suffering and sacrifice (as in *Oedipus* or *King Lear*), so the protagonist in a psychodrama undergoes a kind of self-sacrifice that transforms the whole psychological system. As Jung (1952, p. 429) puts it in *Symbols of Transformation*, "The essence and motive force of the sacrificial drama consist in an unconscious transformation of energy of which the ego becomes aware in much the same way as sailors are made aware of a volcanic upheaval under the sea." A prevailing conscious attitude that was creating much suffering is sacrificed for the sake of a larger dimension of reality, an admission of unconscious forces. King Lear only finds the truth of his egotism when he loses all and goes mad. He becomes as a child and learns to "see feelingly." Estelle Weinrib (1983, pp. 44–45) says that "the very act of playing is a submission of the autonomous ego to the service of creative imagination, the feeling and forming power of the self. Playing requires an attitude or a condition of relatedness to the inner nonrational playful impulse and a willingness to give it concrete expression." The ego holds on to its conscious day-world power. It does not like the idea of a conjunction with its dark side. However, in allowing a union of opposites, of conscious and unconscious, an energy is often released, an opus begins to take place, and an alchemical transformation begins.

Mention should be made of the psychoeducative value of the role playing, and especially of role reversal. Role playing allows the adult to go beyond enclosed egocentric points of view and actually consider in some depth what it feels like to be in another's shoes. Adam Blatner (Blatner and Blatner, 1988, p. 108), says, "The actual process of thinking about another person's role repertoire requires a mixture of imagination and rational exploration. This is the way the legendary Sherlock Holmes worked. He imagined a variety of possible scenarios and then used his logic to test out their probability . . . he allowed images to form spontaneously, and he remained receptive to this intuitional process." In this way, the actual circumstances of significant others can begin taking on a reality that is denied when we are stuck in subjective limitations, with all the projections and distorted fictions contained therein. Entering into a role involves an imaginative test that can lead to mastery. Not all persons in a psychodrama group will become stage actors, but the experience of learning to see with another's eyes can open a world of expressiveness that allows a person to become a kind of practicing dramatist. The skills learned can empower persons to think more broadly about their own creative abilities and the complexity of their own personalities.

The psychodrama format is in keeping with the modern idea of experiential learning, the great pioneering spirit of which was no doubt John Dewey, who wrote the following in 1935:

> If one attempts to formulate the philosophy of education implicit in the practices of the new education, we may, I think, discover certain common principles. . . . To imposition from above as opposed to expression and cultivation of individuality; to external discipline as opposed to free activity; to learning from text and teachers, learning through experience; to acquisition of isolated skills and techniques by drill as opposed to acquisition of them as a means of attaining ends which make direct vital appeal; to preparation for a more or less remote future as opposed to making the most of the opportunities of present life; to static aims and materials as opposed to acquaintance with a changing world.
>
> I take it that the fundamental unity of the newer philosophy is found in the idea that there is an intimate and necessary relation between the processes of actual experience and education [pp. 19-20].

Relationship to Learning

The psychodrama workshop supplies a method that puts the learner in direct contact with the phenomenon being studied, in this case, the individual student. The living interest of the adult student is deeply involved in personal histories, in who they are and where they have been, in what they can do and what they want to do. The individual (paradoxically within a group context) has the opportunity to regain a sense of autonomy in the ways psychodrama uses the imagination. The years of experience that have shaped the psyche of the individual are dramatic interplays subjected to a new freedom, or, as Husserl (1973, p. 382) puts it, "In the realm of the imagination's arbitrary freedom, we can lift all actuality to a plane of pure possibility."

The question may arise of what this realm of pure possibility or freedom from strict boundaries offers the adult learner. It is nothing less than a kind of triumph for the student to enter a realm that was heretofore thought of as out of bounds. As Edward Casey (1976, p. 233) states, "For it is by autonomous imagining that consciousness comes to know itself in its multifariousness—in the diversity of its digressions and the variety of its vicissitudes. In imagining, the mind moves in many ways. Imagination multiplies mentation and is its freest form of movement. It is mind in its polymorphic profusion. It is also mind in the process of self-completion and as such includes an element of self enchantment." He goes on to quote from W. B. Yeats's "The Circus Animals' Desertion":

Heart-mysteries there, and yet all is said
It was the dream itself enchanted me. . . .
Players and painted stage took all my love,
And not those things that they were emblems of.
Those masterful images because complete
Grew in pure mind

And so the imaginative realm of the personal drama can become an arena not only of instruction and the exploration of growth and new freedom but also of pure delight. It is the inducement of these possibilities that perhaps shall be our guide into further awareness of just how the imaginative and the cognitive meet on a very human stage indeed.

References

Blatner, A., and Blatner, A. *Foundations of Psychodrama*. New York: Springer, 1988.

Buber, M. *Between Man and Man*. New York: Macmillan, 1985.

Casey, E. S. *Imagining: A Phenomenological Study*. Bloomington: Indiana University Press, 1976.

Dewey, J. *Experience and Education*. New York: Kappa Delta Pi, 1935.

Goldman, M. *The Actor's Freedom*. New York: Simon & Schuster, 1975.

Hillman, J. *Re-Visioning Psychology*. New York: Harper & Row, 1975.

Husserl, E. *Experience and Judgment*. Evanston, Ill.: Northwestern University Press, 1973.

Jung, C. G. *Symbols of Transformation*. Vol. 5. In G. Adler and others (eds.), *Collected Works*, (R.F.C. Hull, trans.). Princeton, N.J.: Princeton University Press, 1954. (Originally published 1916.)

Jung, C. G. *The Archetypes of the Collective Unconscious*. Vol. 9, Pt. 1. In G. Adler and others (eds.), *Collected Works*, (R.F.C. Hull, trans.). Princeton, N.J.: Princeton University Press, 1954. (Originally published 1916.)

Jung, C. G. *The Structure and Dynamics of the Psyche*. Vol. 8. In G. Adler and others (eds.), *Collected Works*, (R.F.C. Hull, trans.). Princeton, N.J.: Princeton University Press, 1959. (Originally published 1916.)

Polyani, M., and Prosch, H. *Meaning*. Chicago: University of Chicago Press, 1975.

Smith, K., and Berg, D. N. *Paradoxes of Group Life: Understanding Conflict, Paralysis, and Movement in Group Dynamics*. San Francisco: Jossey-Bass, 1987.

Weinrib, E. L. *Images of the Self*. Boston: Sigo Press, 1983.

William D. Pearlman is a professional actor and Jungian-oriented therapist. He is an adjunct professor at Ottawa University, Phoenix Center.

Innovative doctoral programs based on a knowledge and awareness of the multifaceted roles adults play are relatively few and far between.

Many Lives to Lead: The Adult Professional's Quest

J. Bruce Francis

More than a hundred years ago, from a house he designed and built himself on the shores of Walden Pond, Henry David Thoreau ([1854] 1941) described the insights wrought from his period of introspection. What he wrote strikes us today as characteristically adult. It reflects the common experience of highly educated and accomplished professionals who, after the struggles of establishing their careers, become aware of opportunities and challenges beyond those of everyday practice. Political involvement, consulting, travel, artistic pursuits, and even social activism—these are the rewards of professional achievement and at the same time the intellectual and motivational challenges that require dedicated preparation. To prepare for such extraprofessional activities and even to fulfill personal ambitions that career success has not realized, professionals are drawn to advanced education.

It is important to understand that midcareer professionals seek advanced education for very different reasons than do their younger counterparts. Certainly the desire to enhance and upgrade professional training and credentials motivates some, but there are other motivations that lead midcareer adults to seek out advanced study. Among these, three are prominent.

1. *Career change.* Professionals often find themselves, after years of successful practice, being asked to take on managerial responsibilities in an agency they have served. They quickly discover that managing other professionals and support staff requires far different skills and knowledge than does direct service. Such activities as planning, budgeting, and organizing suddenly require knowledge and technique of a different though

no less important kind. They see in advanced education a way to supplement on-the-job training and to establish an added credential.

2. *Personal fulfillment.* Professionals who began their practice with master's degrees at a time when that degree was considered the prime practitioner degree and who have built a successful professional career without having attained the doctorate nevertheless may yearn to achieve it. They do not need it for licensing or even for professional acceptance, but they see it nevertheless as an intellectual capstone, a form of recognition that has intrinsic merit, signifying the attainment of knowledge at the highest level.

3. *Social involvement.* As practitioners gain experience and enter the stages of life when motivations beyond career take precedence, their desire to view their own profession from a broader perspective becomes more and more important. To see their work in the context of social and cultural values, to consider the effects on their profession of changes in the society, and to consider how their profession might change society— these are important motivations for advanced professionals. As they contemplate the enormous problems their profession faces both now and in the future, their own need to know more, to study the foundations of their profession, and to develop the intellectual perspectives that can only come from a multidisciplinary orientation make advanced education an increasingly higher priority.

Recognizing this need of advanced professionals, some institutions of higher education have in recent years begun to alter their structures and patterns to accommodate a different kind of student, one whose developmental needs change as the years move on. As Maehl (1987) has pointed out, the external doctorate is one response to the challenge of developing advanced educational opportunities for midcareer adults. It provides midcareer, fully employed adults a chance to advance their professional qualifications and at the same time to integrate that change with issues of midlife professional development.

While more and more traditional institutions have begun to recognize the needs of advanced adult learners and to modify their curricula and teaching approaches to accommodate them, it has remained for a few alternative institutions to devote their full attention to this segment of the population.

Walden University, a freestanding national doctoral institution based in Minneapolis, Minnesota, is one such institution with educational programs that are different from those of traditional schools, programs motivated by a distinctive philosophy, constituency, and history. From its earliest days in 1970, Walden made the commitment to serve adult professionals who were deserving of doctoral study but for whom opportunities on a doctoral level were limited. It sought from the beginning to develop its academic program to meet the needs of adult learners seeking graduate study related to their professions, and to do so in a context that enabled them to continue full-time professional activity.

Utilizing a knowledge of adult development theory, Walden University began with the philosophy that adult professionals learn in ways different from those of entry-level students. Experienced adults have established professional commitments, leadership roles in their communities and professional organizations, and learning histories supplemented by experience that becomes the new base for doctoral study. Professional and leadership roles comprise the learning environment for the mid-career student. The campus experience, in turn, becomes a series of short-term, intensive periods for designing learning programs, acquiring new knowledge or skills, and receiving assessments in learning.

Recent research on adult learning (Suanmali, as cited in Brookfield, 1986) has generated certain principles of self-directed learning that include the following suggestions for educators:

1. Progressively decrease the learner's dependency on faculty

2. Help the learner to understand how to use learning resources

3. Help the learner to define her or his learning needs

4. Help the learner to assume increased responsibility for defining, planning, and evaluating his or her own learning

5. Organize what is to be learned in relationship to the student's current problems, concerns, and level of understanding

6. Foster learner decision making: select learning experiences that require choosing, expand the learner's range of options, and facilitate appreciation for the perspectives of others who have alternative ways of understanding

7. Encourage the use of criteria for judging that are increasingly inclusive and differentiating in awareness while remaining self-reflective and integrative of experience

8. Facilitate problem posing and problem solving, especially in the areas of individual and collective action and those that concern the relationship between personal problems and public issues

9. Reinforce the learner's self-concept by providing for progressive mastery

10. Emphasize experiential, participative, and projective instructional methods with appropriate use of modeling and learning contracts.

These principles have implications for the design of alternative degree programs at all levels. Adult learners are self-directed; their overall learning need is to attend to advanced competence rather than to entry-level mastery. As adult professionals with career histories, they see college degrees not only as an opportunity to enter a profession but also as an opportunity to reach the higher realms of the profession they are already in and to satisfy a personal sense of accomplishment. As mature adults with families and established lives, they are connected to learning environments and resources that can be used for study. As middle-aged leaders, they want and benefit from a fresh view of their professions amidst personal and societal change.

Walden's programs, like those at similar institutions such as Fielding Institute and the Union Institute for Graduate Study, build on professional and personal competence and enhance that competence through scholarly inquiry and the advancement of knowledge in matters of societal significance. Dispersed educational resources and programs provide opportunities to mature adults whose professional responsibilities, established families, and individual learning styles make attendance at traditional institutions difficult if not impossible. Competency assessments of learning outcomes enable practicing professionals to demonstrate doctoral-level knowledge and to carry out scholarship equivalent to that of traditional graduate programs. Because each adult learner's program evolves differently, the relationships between faculty and students are collegial. Faculty are mentors, role models, facilitators of educational outcomes.

Institutions such as Walden seek to help adult learners understand themselves in terms of adult developmental stages in the context of change. Lifelong learning is also a perpetual ingredient in life planning and career development. While adults need to be specialists in a professional area, their fundamental need for the management of changes within themselves and society at large is integrated, multidisciplinary, holistic knowledge. Walden seeks to integrate professional understanding with the knowledge of change and to foster scholar-practitioners who can both increase their knowledge and utilize that knowledge in new applications, leading to new and renewed social commitments in their lives and professions.

The Walden Program

Walden offers the doctor of philosophy and the doctor of education degrees. The Ph.D. degree is offered in the following multidisciplinary tracks.

Administration/Management. This area of study focuses on the concepts and skills necessary to foster and guide the survival, growth, and development of goal-directed organizations and institutions. Students who select this track are primarily from government, business, and public agencies. The content spans information, communication, needs analysis, organizational design, leadership, problem solving, and decision making. The associated disciplines and fields that inform the area include the social and political sciences, economics, human resource management, and information science.

Adult professionals considering a move into the management of social agencies, into the expansion and diversification of their own professional corporations, or into governmental agencies may find opportunities in the administration/management track to develop their knowledge and skills in planning and organizing, which will prepare them for managing more complex organizations.

Education. This area of study focuses on the concepts and skills necessary to transmit knowledge to individuals and groups. Students who select this track are primarily teachers and curriculum designers in schools, colleges, public agencies, and businesses. The curriculum spans learning theory, techniques of educational design and delivery, and the processes of educational planning and evaluation. Associated disciplines and fields include the social and behavioral sciences, communications, and education.

Human Services. This program focuses on the concepts and skills necessary to improve the human condition through planned interventions in the psychological and social problems of individuals and groups in society. Students selecting this track are typically professionals in public and private agencies providing psychological and social services to individuals and families. The curriculum spans psychology, social work, community organization, and social planning.

Health Services. This program focuses on the concepts and skills necessary to protect health and to plan, develop, and deliver health care to individuals and groups. Students pursuing this track are typically professionals in nursing, health planning, medical technology, and epidemiology. The curriculum spans health care systems and techniques, care for and prevention of diseases, including etiology, treatment, and concepts of wellness. Adult professionals can use study in Walden's health services' track to probe more deeply the theoretical underpinnings of their practice and to extend their understanding of the societal variables that affect the behavior and attitudes of their clients.

Admission to the Walden doctoral program is based on a careful review of each candidate's potential to complete the program of choice successfully. Faculty analysis of an individual portfolio serves to appraise each applicant's background and potential. Admission is typically granted to applicants who have a master's degree or its equivalent and three or more years of professional experience. Applicants who demonstrate readiness to begin doctoral study are invited to attend an admissions workshop, where final admissions decisions are made by faculty members.

Admitted students in all tracks progress through the program by completing the following academic requirements, which together are designed to build on professional experience and extend it to areas of academic specialization:

1. *The professional development plan* describes and analyzes past academic and professional achievements, current strengths and weaknesses, and professional goals.

2. *The preliminary proposal* organizes the topic area of the dissertation, explores the various elements that make up a high-quality dissertation, and provides a framework for further development of knowledge on which the dissertation will be based.

3. *The core knowledge area modules* are demonstrations of doctoral-level knowledge in four general areas based on learning contracts negotiated with faculty. The core modules enable the student to demonstrate knowledge of the intellectual scope and quality of the final dissertation proposal.

4. *The final proposal* is a blueprint for the dissertation, incorporating the theoretical and methodological decisions that narrow and focus the research project.

5. *The advanced knowledge area modules* are demonstrations of knowledge in three advanced specialization areas related to the target profession. Through the advanced modules students demonstrate understanding of theory and practice in the profession and the ability to apply that knowledge to specific issues and problems that affect the profession in its relation to society.

6. *The dissertation* is the final phase of study for Walden doctoral students. It involves carrying out an independent research study and writing a detailed descriptive report. Walden encourages flexible but rigorous research designs. Each student arranges a final oral presentation of his or her completed dissertation.

Walden's focus on principles of adult learning and development has led to the development of unusual approaches to certain fundamental dimensions of doctoral study. These include a dispersed residency, collegial relations between faculty and students, an outcomes-based learning model, and a comprehensive system for evaluating and tracking student progress.

Dispersed Residency

Throughout the history of graduate education, residency has provided an opportunity for faculty and students to become a community of scholars. Traditionally this has meant that students have lived on or near a campus, but today more diverse opportunities are available and necessary to accommodate adult learners. Dispersed residency represents the multiple contact points among students and faculty as they together participate in a network for learning and evaluation throughout the program. It is not of less value than campus-based residency; it is simply different in that it is constructed in a broader social milieu and operates more on the basis of student initiative.

Walden's dispersed residency is administered as an extended network of services, from which students design their program with support and guidance. Walden's main office in Minneapolis functions as the hub of the network. Although the Walden program emphasizes self-directed learning, it is important for students to work closely with faculty on designing their programs and organizing their learning activities as well as in having their knowledge assessed. Such faculty-student contact takes a variety of forms in order to supplement the student's independent work, to provide sufficient opportunity for corrective feedback when necessary, and to establish a basis for continuing scholarly interaction. Walden has created a series of faculty-student contact points available to students throughout the year. These educational services are offered through intensive sessions, local clusters, individual meetings and conversations, and computer communication. Throughout the year, students take advantage of whichever services they choose, but they must participate in at least one three-week summer intensive session during their program and two regional intensive sessions per year.

The intensive sessions are held in conference centers and are offered in Minnesota during the summer and in several locations in various parts of the country each quarter, depending on student needs. At the intensive sessions students participate in formal lectures, small-group seminars, and individual tutorials on the subject matter of the knowledge area modules and on principles and techniques of research design. In addition, they work individually with faculty to develop and refine learning/assessment contracts, to review progress, and to plan future work.

Resources available to students include guides for writing the professional development plan and the knowledge area modules and materials useful in the development of the dissertation proposal and dissertation. Each knowledge area module has a curriculum guide to provide overviews for adult learners as they conduct their studies and arrange for knowledge assessments. Each module directs students to primary readings, basic concepts and theories, historical background and current trends, and the criteria whereby knowledge related to the module is assessed.

Walden students carry out research and dissertation writing in their home environment, making use of appropriate research resources available in graduate libraries. Periodically, Walden secures statements of accessibility from other local and regional libraries to assist its students. This access is supplemented by personal and professional agency libraries.

During the dissertation-writing period Walden provides orientation and direct assistance to students in deciding what resources are needed, makes students aware of the availability of appropriate resources and the means to access them, makes clear to students the importance of adequate library work, and provides special assistance for those for whom access is difficult.

Collegial Relations with Students

Student learning is guided by a doctoral committee with extensive experience, knowledge of adults as learners, and high levels of professional attainment, including substantial records of research and publication. The doctoral committee includes (1) a faculty adviser who serves as overall mentor, broker of learning resources, assessor of certain knowledge area modules, and chair of the dissertation committee; (2) one or more assessors who evaluate the demonstrations of student knowledge in core and advanced knowledge area modules; (3) a faculty reader who serves as an additional evaluator for the proposal and dissertation; and (4) an external consultant/examiner who is selected for expertise in the subject matter of the dissertation and who provides consultative guidance in the professional area and evaluates the final product.

An important element of collegiality is the way faculty evaluations of student work are handled. Walden is committed to the principle that primary responsibility for academic evaluation of student work rests on the judgment of qualified faculty. The systems seek to buttress that judgment by establishing clear and common criteria known to students in advance, on which faculty will make their judgments. Walden also maintains detailed records of the bases for faculty judgments. These are available to students and are reviewed by appropriate academic authorities to ensure both fairness to students and common interpretation of institutional criteria.

Outcomes-Based Learning Model

Doctoral-level study requires mastery of broad conceptual and historical knowledge, in-depth understanding of theoretical and practical issues, and the ability to apply knowledge to problems of professional significance. Walden students acquire and demonstrate these competencies through completion of a series of knowledge area modules (KAMs). The unifying goal of the KAM program is to provide an effective vehicle whereby students can acquire and demonstrate doctoral-level competence.

Throughout the KAM program there is an emphasis on integrating contemporary theory with professional practice and on understanding the bilateral relationship between professional practice and change. The larger context in which adults live and work shapes their professional experience in ways often unexpected; at the same time, their work within that social system can transform the system itself.

The KAM program is based on four core KAMs to be completed by all students and three advanced KAMs specific to each professional track. The four core KAMs explore societal development and the future; human development; organizational and social systems; and research design, analysis, and theory. The rationale for selecting these topics has several bases.

1. The core KAMs reflect faculty conceptions of the kinds of knowledge needed by advanced professionals to critique their everyday activities in the light of broader principles derived from intellectual traditions. Thus, students are helped to better understand general principles of how human mental and emotional processes work (development), how organizations and institutions work (systems), how societies work (societal development and the future), and how the fundamental processes of intellectual inquiry work (research and theory).

2. The core KAMs reflect the sources of information that advanced professionals use to analyze their situations and make judgments. These sources of information are people (development), institutions and groups (systems), and society at large (societal development and the future). The KAM on research focuses on the process of acquiring knowledge from a variety of sources in a systematic way.

3. The core KAMs reflect Walden's orientation to change in the professions and to the concern that students are prepared to pursue their professions in a constantly changing environment. Thus, an awareness of change has been incorporated into all of the KAMs. The KAM on people is oriented toward their development, the KAM on groups and institutions is oriented toward the theoretical principles that best comprehend change (systems), and the KAM on society is oriented toward an awareness of changes in the future and to principles of ecological balance as the changes occur. The research KAM provides a basis for understanding real changing phenomena by emphasizing field and laboratory research, policy-oriented and theory-oriented research, and change-oriented research as well as studies of static phenomena.

The first advanced KAM in each professional track focuses on theoretical issues in the profession, while the second generally compares contemporary professional practices and strategies. The third advanced KAM in each professional track provides guidelines for a case study/practicum experience.

The KAMs provide a common conceptual framework and a standard of competence for all Walden students. At the same time they allow enough flexibility to ensure a high degree of personal and professional relevance. Students use the KAMs to develop the foundation knowledge and skills needed to complete the dissertation and to facilitate their empowerment as agents of social and professional change. The KAMs are self-paced and are designed with adult learning styles in mind.

Each KAM consists of three components: breadth, depth, and application. The breadth of knowledge component requires a demonstration of familiarity with the broad theoretical and conceptual underpinnings of the knowledge base. The assignments allow for individually designed approaches but are based on essentially the same cross-disciplinary literature. The depth of knowledge component entails a demonstration of understanding of the latest thinking in the profession regarding a particular aspect of each knowledge area. Students develop an annotated bibliography and write a scholarly paper that reflects a "state-of-the-art" understanding of the profession's issues and concerns. In the application component, the student either develops a project especially for this KAM or submits a previously completed project along with a five-to-seven-page statement explaining how the project demonstrates the ability to apply the contents of the knowledge area to a professional role.

The components of each KAM share a common internal structure. Learning objectives for the component are set forth, and a list of basic readings is provided. Students select a specified number of these titles, the contents of which are integrated in a comprehensive assignment. This assignment is either selected from a series of options or individually developed in consultation with the adviser. Each KAM also includes appendixes that review criteria for assessment, suggest questions and issues for consideration, and provide extensive supplementary bibliographies.

Assessment of the KAMs is based on how clearly the student demonstrates and expresses competence. The emphasis in all cases is on written, scholarly communication. Papers produced for each component (breadth, depth, and application) of each KAM are equivalent in scope and rigor to what would be required in a three-credit doctoral seminar. Papers must also show evidence of conceptualization that involves comparison and contrast of the ideas found in the literature. Students are encouraged to make the work they do for the KAMs relevant to their jobs and to their prospective doctoral research projects.

Student Tracking System

Theories of adult learning place great premium on the initiative and self-motivation of students. What is not always so clearly understood is that adult learners, particularly those engaged in full-time pursuit of their profession, may often be distracted from their academic work by day-to-day activities. In addition, if students are engaged in long-distance learning, they may become isolated in their work and not have an easy way to gain access to the support systems that a campus might more readily afford them. The consequences of such distraction and isolation may interfere with an adult learner's progress and may even lead to withdrawal from the program. It is therefore particularly important for an institution with an alternative delivery system to develop extraordinary means for keeping track of how its adult learners are progressing.

The Walden tracking system uses both manual and computer means to record, monitor, and analyze the progress of each student through the program. A record is kept for each student of the dates on which each program milestone is reached. Every two weeks a status summary report is generated and reviewed by the dean. This review enables the dean to identify (1) students who do not show sufficient progress and (2) process problems such as failure to follow procedures and proper academic sequences, self-processing, and inordinate delays in communication.

A special computer system analyzes the tracking record for each student and compares that student's progress with fifteen criteria established as appropriate for normal progress through the program. The computer flags instances of discrepancy from those criteria and compiles a weighted problem score for each student. These weighted scores generate for each student a list and a descriptive summary, which are reviewed by the dean.

Formal written progress reports are required each term from both student and adviser. The student report asks the student to describe his or her activities during that month, to indicate what progress has been made, and to specify any problems for which assistance is needed. The faculty report asks the faculty adviser to evaluate the progress of the student during the past term and to alert the dean to any problems for which the faculty adviser might seek assistance. The dean reviews the reports, checking particularly for discrepancies between the student's evaluation of progress and the faculty adviser's evaluation. Reports trigger either a letter of encouragement or a telephone call from the dean, depending on what the student needs.

The entire system is labor intensive but is believed to be a major factor in anticipating and preempting academic problems, in helping students maintain high levels of motivation, and in addressing some of the causes of adult student dropout. All student progress, the provision of all resources, and the candidate assessments are monitored by means of the Walden tracking system. This comprehensive record-keeping system ensures that all candidates are in regular contact with the institution, are kept informed of all matters that concern them, and are provided the means to solve problems that arise.

Conclusion

Thoreau's sojourn at Walden Pond, alluded to at the outset of the chapter, was relatively brief, but it had a profound effect on him and, through his writing about it, on succeeding generations of questioning adults. His description (Thoreau, [1854] 1941, p. 343) of why he left strikes a responsive chord in the adult learner: "I left the woods for as good a reason as I went there. Perhaps it seemed to me that I had several more lives to live."

Adult learners are established adults, with families and jobs, with career identities and financial resources. They know how to locate and find learning resources and how to collaborate. As mature and established professional practitioners, they have already acquired knowledge at the graduate level, may have already published scholarly and professional papers, and hold positions of distinction in their fields. They are largely self-motivated and accustomed to achievement and are eager to produce works of scholarly substance and significance, attain a doctorate, and move on to new opportunities and horizons.

Since its founding, Walden has sought to serve such students, whom more conventional graduate schools were reluctant to admit to doctoral study. As demographic trends bring about the aging of the general population, and as demands for knowledge increase in society, the need for services to adult learners can only increase. Walden, along with other adult-oriented institutions, steeped in the principles of adult development, plays a vital part in helping to nurture and recognize an important societal resource.

References

Brookfield, S. D. *Understanding and Facilitating Adult Learning: A Comprehensive Analysis of Principles and Effective Practices.* San Francisco: Jossey-Bass, 1986.

Maehl, W. H. "The Advanced Adult Learner: A New Challenge for Professional Education." *Minnesota Psychologist,* Fall 1987.

Thoreau, H. D. *Walden.* New York: Norton, 1941. (Originally published 1854.)

J. Bruce Francis is academic vice-president for Walden University.

Adults returning to learning bring a wealth of untapped resources in the form of their personal experiences. This wealth needs to be used rather than neglected.

The Proseminar

Daniel L. Foxx, Jr.

Ottawa University is but one of many institutions determined to provide a comprehensive and effective degree program for adults (see Chapter Four for another example of an institution granting doctoral degrees to adults and utilizing a nontraditional, adult-oriented delivery system). In Ottawa's two adult centers, in Kansas City, Kansas and in Phoenix, Arizona, the challenges also become important learning experiences. The discoveries of such adult learning researchers as Erikson, Havighurst, Perry, Kohlberg, Loevinger, and others became the foundation for Ottawa's approach to working with adults. Recognizing from past research and from continuous experience that adults learn differently than do traditional-aged students, adult educators at Ottawa developed the Proseminar.

Adults as Learners

The traditional view that college is for the young has been effectively dismissed in the last decade. In 1987, 16 percent of all college students were over the age of thirty-five (Brandt, 1989). Further, more than six million college students are over twenty-five years of age. It is safe to say that older students will be in the majority by the year 2000. This information presents academe with some serious challenges, not the least of which is how to respond to a growing clientele that not only requires but also demands that its unique needs be met. The heart of the challenge can be summed up in a single question: What methods are effective in teaching adults?

A reasonable starting point could be to understand why adults return to college in the first place. A forty-five-year-old who had just enrolled in a college course for the first time in twenty-five years was hoping, in part, for a change of careers: "When I first started looking for a job just out of high school, I was asked by every interviewer, 'Are you a high school graduate?' Now everyone wants to know if I hold an advanced degree. That seems to say to me that a bachelor's degree is about as good today as a high school diploma was twenty-five years ago."

If this is true, we can also expect a rush of adult learners to the nation's graduate schools. But what about those who find themselves in the same boat with the forty-five-year-old above? Should they be interested in a college degree program solely for job security?

Recent research indicates that there are additional and diverse reasons for the interest and that workplace marketability might actually be a low priority. There is growing pressure on nondegreed employees at every level of business, industry, and government to take steps to validate their positions with a college degree. Many persons who are in midlevel and other responsible positions and have seniority with their companies also feel this pressure.

A story frequently heard by those who advise adult learners was repeated again in an academic planning session between an adult student and his adviser: "I thought I was so talented to have moved up to a responsible job with my company in only five years even though I did not have a college degree. I have to admit that I had become pretty smug as I watched others who had struggled through college working for me, and for much less money."

The situation had changed suddenly and drastically for this student just a few weeks before that conversation took place. The student's company had been acquired in a merger by a group that required a degreed person to fill his position. The new policy allowed him only eighteen months to acquire the needed degree.

While the two students described above have employment-related reasons for returning to college, the most frequently stated reason is self-satisfaction. One sixty-two-year-old man attending his first college course in over forty years said, "I just got too busy to finish something I started a long time ago, but I've owed myself this for a long time. I want my kids to know that I can do it."

Adults, then, approach education for a variety of reasons, most of which are very pragmatic and goal specific. Many are returning to the classroom after long absences spent raising a family or climbing the corporate ladder. Others are taking college courses for the first time. Whatever their personal reasons, most adults feel apprehensive and are plagued by self-doubts.

Those feelings are very real for adults in a society that, for years, has been centered around youth. Many wonder if it is possible to "teach an old dog new tricks," and they worry about failure in their studies. For the majority of adults seeking a college degree, that first step is made at great personal risk to their self-image. A comfortable transition is in order, an orientation or warm-up, to adult learning.

Proseminar: A Return to Learning

The first course that all entering students take at Ottawa University's adult centers is one answer to these needs. Called Proseminar, it is the basic general education course in the Ottawa University degree program. The Proseminar engages the adult student in learning and skill development that contribute to the accomplishment of individual educational goals in the context of Ottawa's degree requirements.

The Proseminar is a multipurpose course designed to orient students to the Ottawa program and to help them make a meaningful transition to college-level studies as adults. As the students progress through the eight-week course, the different aspects of the Ottawa program are explained in detail. Since adults are usually on campus only for class meetings, it is important that they understand early the administrative policies that will affect them as students (for example, registration, procedures, financial aid, withdrawal from classes).

Of more immediate importance to the students' success, however, are matters relating to their learning. A primary objective of the course is to engage students in group interaction and critical thinking through issues related to adult development, self-assessment, and goals development.

Ottawa places great emphasis on the advisement process and introduces the student to his or her adviser through the Proseminar. The person who teaches the Proseminar becomes the adviser for the students in the class. The full-time faculty at the centers take turns teaching the Proseminar and typically teach two Proseminars each year, giving the faculty a constantly changing pool of advisees with whom they work. For the student this aspect of the program can create a sense of security and continuity, as the person with whom they begin their degree program stays with them throughout their studies. The continuity and the advisement process are the heart of the Ottawa adult program.

The relationship between the adviser and the student is intended to be a proactive one, and it is frequently a surprise to new students to learn that the person teaching their first course will be such an important part of their academic careers. One student remarked that her understanding of academic advisement until she began the Proseminar was suggestive of planned failure. "I always got a card at the beginning of the semester telling me the name of my adviser. The card instructed me to contact him if I had any problems," she said. "Since I didn't want to admit to having problems, I never contacted him."

This problem is less likely to happen in the Ottawa program because of the close relationship established between student and adviser during the Proseminar. The adviser often initiates contact throughout the student's stay at Ottawa to offer encouragement and guidance. This relationship carries through to graduation, where the adviser plays a role in the graduation ceremonies.

The material and the information covered in the Proseminar are designed, among other things, to establish and strengthen this important student-adviser relationship. Required readings cover such topics as adult learning, communication, goal setting, and values. Written assignments require the student to react to the ideas and concepts in the reading material in order to encourage critical thinking. Open discussion in class engages the students in group interaction and critical thinking through issues related to adult development, self-assessment, and goals development.

In dealing with adults in group discussion and other exercises that require interaction within the group, it is important to conduct the session so as to lessen students' fears or anxieties about speaking out. Recognizing these adult anxieties with humor and sincere warmth can help to develop a comfortable atmosphere in the classroom that allays many of these feelings and encourages participation.

Not all students feel comfortable about speaking out at first. Creating a sense of community in the classroom is desirable and can be achieved in a number of ways. One reliable method is some form of personal introduction, but it must be done carefully.

I usually begin the Proseminar with a story about an early teaching experience when I used the introductory icebreaker without giving any thought to the ramifications. In my inexperience I announced that we would go around the classroom and have the students introduce themselves to everyone in the class. The first person to introduce himself chose to stand, although I had not made that a requirement. Following his lead, each student stood in turn and introduced himself or herself. When it came the turn of a young woman sitting near the center of the class, she stood, took a deep breath in preparation, and then fainted.

I then explain to my Proseminar class that the purpose of introductions is not to embarrass anyone, and I make it clear that no one need participate unless they want to. The idea, after all, is to create a feeling of comfort while encouraging the students to make that first step to participation in class discussions. To make it easier, I give the students a list of statements in order to help them prepare their introductions (see Exhibit 1).

It is critical for the student to come to an understanding of self in the context of adult learning. The major product of the Proseminar,

Exhibit 1. Preparation for Self-Introductions

To Help You with Your Introduction

Name: _____

1. What I do:
2. My family consists of (wife/husband, children, pets):
3. Things I like:
4. Things I don't like:
5. What brought me back to college at this stage of my life:
6. What I plan to study or major in (if decided):
7. Someday I would like to (or if "someday" sounds too uncertain, try "before I die I would like to"):

therefore, is an exercise called the learning autobiography (LAB), which asks the student to write about himself or herself as a learner on six main topics dealing with formal and informal learning, significant learning events, important people in the student's learning, and personal philosophy and goals. (This is more fully developed in Chapter Six.) This exercise has a twofold purpose. First, the student has the opportunity to develop a better understanding of personal learning strengths and weaknesses and to formulate learning strategies based on that knowledge. Second, the answers to the questions posed in the LAB help the adviser to be more effective in assisting the student to develop an appropriate and meaningful educational plan.

Many adults bring vast amounts of personal experience to their studies. This experience is viable and valuable and may have many applications to the student's degree program. Another purpose of the Proseminar is to assist students in a process of assessing their prior learning, skills and knowledge, values, and goals. Some of the learning that the student has acquired outside the classroom through on-the-job training or experience, informal study, or seminars and workshops may have academic value when properly evaluated. The assessment of prior learning that begins in the Proseminar may lead to a formal process of evaluation and assessment that could result in the awarding of academic credit that can be applied toward degree requirements.

During the Proseminar, the initial process of identifying the learning that the student has acquired takes place. One exercise required of all students is completing "activity reports." These reports help the adult learner to evaluate and list all learning, formal as well as informal, under four headings known as the breadth competencies. These are communication, social/civic responsibilities, lifelong learning, and values. Students prepare one report for each of these four competencies. All learning related to each topic is listed as either college credit from formal courses or from life/work experience. Exhibit 2 is an example of a communication activities report.

Exhibit 2. Breadth Activities Report (Communication)

I.   Activities I report in this area include the following:

A.   Formal courses

ENG 101	Freshmen English	6 hrs.	A
ENG 102	Composition and literature	3	C
SPE 211	Public speaking	3	B
SPA 116	Conversational Spanish	3	B
ENG 230	Research and report writing	3	B
SDR 103	Interpersonal communication	4	B

B.   Learning from life/work experience
   • Attending a three-day workshop on grants and proposal writing for my department and writing an unsuccessful grant proposal
   • Preparing a position paper for my department on evaluation of performance by peers and supervisors
   • Presenting a lecture on two new techniques at a regional meeting of my professional association
   • Writing a draft of a speech for my supervisor to deliver
   • Organizing a three-day conference for persons in my professional association from a five-state area, including planning, advance publicity, speaker selection, writing of program brochure, and conducting evaluation sessions
   • Spending four months in Mexico and being able to make my way with native speakers of Spanish without resorting to English
   • Teaching a one-week course (three hours each day) for persons in my company on career goal setting and resume writing
   • Serving as moderator of my local civic club at two luncheons jointly sponsored with the chamber of commerce
   • Attending a one-day workshop on equal employment opportunity laws.

The ability to communicate clearly and effectively is of paramount importance for two reasons. First, such competence is crucial to effective and continued learning and hence to the attainment of degree goals. Second, such competence is also important in living a full and productive life personally, vocationally, and in relations with others. Included in effective communication are oral, written, and interpersonal skills.

Formal courses to be reported in this area might include the following:

Public speaking	Creative writing	Studio arts
Debate	Debate/technical writing	Performing arts
Oral interpretation	Research methods	Interpersonal
Acting	Foreign language	communication
Basic composition	Linguistics/semantics	

Through this exercise the students show, through a combination of formal and informal learning, that they have a breadth of knowledge in each of these areas. One major emphasis in the process is to help students learn to think in terms of integrating all of their learning in each of the areas so that all learning is assumed to be important. If, in reviewing the activity reports, the adviser feels that a sufficient breadth in any area is not demonstrated, a student may be advised to take additional courses in the deficient area(s).

A theme that runs through the Proseminar is mutually negotiated educational planning. Each student is required to complete a formal educational plan that outlines her or his projected coursework and integrates prior learning into the overall plan through the activity reports. The adviser's role in this process is to facilitate, not to dictate. Students are expected to take charge of their planning by thoughtfully choosing courses that reflect their own goals and interests.

Advisers know what is required to make a viable degree program, but beyond that they want to make certain that students take personal responsibility for expressing their own goals. For this reason degree programs are not preplanned. Prospective students are frequently surprised that they are not provided with a list of required courses, but most adults appreciate the self-directed nature of the Ottawa program.

The activity reports help students to classify their informal learning and can also become the basis for claims for college credits that they may later file in a credit-by-assessment portfolio. The process of credit by assessment (CBA) is discussed in some detail in the Proseminar, and basic guidelines are explained. The student learns that the two major criteria for granting a CBA claim for credit are that learning must be at the college level and be related to established college courses and that the learning must be appropriately documented. In other words, the student first identifies informal learning, determines if it is compatible with established college coursework, and then submits the appropriate documentation to verify that he or she does, in fact, know what is claimed in the CBA portfolio.

Self-Evaluation

Self-evaluation or self-exploration is a valuable part of the Proseminar for a number of reasons. Perhaps the most important of these is to help students to take an organized look at their successes and failures, strengths and weaknesses. For many this is a novel idea, one not always readily accepted by students. I introduce this process by telling my students about a friend who signed on as a client of a top-rated employment counseling agency. The fee he paid for services was $4,500, and the first thing he was asked to do was to write his autobiography. My friend's counseling agency was interested in knowing about his strengths and accomplishments in his profession so that they could help to market him to prospective employers.

The difference (besides cost) between my friend's program and what we ask our students to do at Ottawa is that we want our students to concentrate on themselves as learners. Adult developmental theory is most helpful in this regard. It is extremely important that an adult student have certain self-knowledge to be a successful learner. Some of the questions students are encouraged to ask and answer are as follows: How do I learn best? What kinds of learning situations are best for me? What kind of learner am I? Understanding how the answers to these questions affect their learning then enables students to formulate learning strategies for their educational plans and for the future.

Of all the observable outcomes of the Proseminar, perhaps the most impressive is the change in the way the students perceive themselves. This change may not be discernible immediately after the course ends but may come over a period of time as the student puts into practice what has transpired in the Proseminar.

In the first Proseminar I offered, a woman in her early forties was more than mildly resistant to the whole concept. After the first class meeting she approached me and told me that she thought we expected too much and that she did not see any merit in her going any further.

Being new to the Proseminar myself but having a belief in the idea, I tried to reason with her. Finally, I said to her, "If you'll stick it out for three weeks and do the assignments, and if you still feel the same, I'll make other arrangements for you."

I could tell by the expression on her face that I was not making much headway. Then I heard myself say, "However, if you really apply yourself, I think this could even be a spiritual experience for you."

The woman accepted that challenge, but my greatest surprise was what I had said about spiritual experiences. As I pondered it over and over driving home from class that night, I wondered what had possessed me to say such a thing.

After a few days I forgot about the incident, and my student completed the course. She participated in discussions and completed the assignments. After the course ended, she continued with her studies. When she was approaching graduation, she came into my office to discuss her graduation review, a research paper sometimes referred to by students as the senior thesis, and to talk about her progress in some other areas.

As we were concluding our session, she said to me in a serious tone, "You were right." I was not certain what she meant and probably had a puzzled expression on my face. She continued, "Do you remember what you told me in Proseminar? That it could be a spiritual experience?" I nodded. "Well, you were right. When I came back to college, I wasn't sure where I was going. I had been a secretary since I graduated from high school. That's all I had ever really wanted to be, and I was a good secretary. But I never realized until I began to explore what I had learned over the years that I was much more than that. I had management skills. I was a competent communicator. I was capable of making good decisions. The Proseminar helped me put all that in perspective, and it has changed my life. I changed jobs last year, you know. Last week I was promoted to vice-president."

Not all students have such dramatic stories to tell, but we have found that all who pass through the Proseminar receive benefits that serve them not only through their academic studies but also beyond. The concept of accepting adult students as people with valuable experience, capable of learning and going on to integrate the two, can enrich their lives and validate their worth in a changing world.

Applications of the Proseminar Concept

Until recently most of us believed, and the lack of research confirmed, that the last stage in human development ended somewhere between the ages of eighteen and twenty-one. Following the exciting explosion of preteen learning and physical development and the turbulent teenage quest for identity and belonging came the safe harbor of adulthood. In the minds of many the stability and self-assurance of adulthood was a reward for surviving the teen years. It was something that just "comes," much like spring following winter.

There are universal problems and concerns with which all adults struggle. Making changes, whether returning to education, learning a new procedure on the job, or embarking on entirely new careers, creates stress. The feelings of inadequacy and anxiety that an adult can experience upon taking a college course for the first time in years are no less stressful than they are for an adult who makes changes and transitions in any other arena. Adults are often unprepared for these kinds of feelings because they have been programmed to think that adulthood is a nirvana of calm and completeness.

The Proseminar provides several options to help adults make those transitions and deal with the anxieties that change brings. Perhaps one of the most valuable results of a Proseminar approach, with its presentation of adult themes and introduction to the theories of adult learning, is that we learn that these feelings are not at all unique to us as individuals. Sometimes it is comforting to know that while each of us is unique and different in much the same way that no two snowflakes are exactly alike, we are not necessarily alone when we feel anxiety and stress.

The value of the Proseminar concept is that it can be adapted in a variety of ways to meet the needs of different groups. Its techniques have been used with success in both educational and noneducational settings. Self-assessment, goal setting, and advisement are the tools of many trades.

An instructor wishing to adapt the Proseminar should approach the task as would a public speaker, considering first the type of audience to be addressed. The instructor should be flexible enough to change directions if indicated by the needs of the group or in response to the teaching opportunities that may arise in the course of the Proseminar.

While the academic aspects of the Proseminar peculiar to the Ottawa model might not be appropriate in nonacademic settings, the general aims mentioned above have much significance. The philosophy is to assist students as they attempt to understand themselves as learners and to explore the various avenues to learning and self-awareness. The rewards of this enterprise are self-evident.

Reference

Brandt, N. "Adults Return to Education." *USA Today,* September 12, 1989, p. 1.

Daniel L. Foxx, Jr., is assistant professor of history at the
Phoenix Center of Ottawa University.

The learning autobiography helps adults to realize the impact of personal experience on learning and to foster a mentoring relationship.

The Learning Autobiography: A Foundation for Mentoring

Callistus W. Milan

As related in Chapter Five, the keystone of the Ottawa University adult degree program is the Proseminar. This course provides opportunities for the reentry adult student to assess educational and vocational goals, resurrect some of the skills that may have been dormant for some time, and engage in critical thinking and academic dialogue. Research concerning adults as learners indicates that this group of learners needs a supportive environment, a fact not overlooked by the planners of the Proseminar. The format of the Proseminar, the approach of the facilitator (instructor) of the course, class subject matter, and participation blend together to give the adult student comfort and ease in reentering the college environment.

Especially noteworthy in this entire process is the role of the facilitator. The facilitator/instructor takes on a multiplicity of activities: a builder of confidence in the students, an assessor of students' strengths and weaknesses, an adviser in students' academic program development, and a catalyst in the evolution of a mentoring relationship with students. Being cognizant of these roles, the facilitator/instructor constructs the Proseminar to accomplish these goals. The successful attainment of some of these goals is immediately apparent—the assessment of the strengths and weaknesses of the student and the development of an educational plan. More remote in nature is the establishment of a mentor relationship. Most collegiate institutions and departments provide academic advisers. Graduation requirements, selective electives, and major courses are the usual discussion items when the traditional student and the faculty adviser meet. This is hardly a mentoring relationship. Lea

NEW DIRECTIONS FOR ADULT AND CONTINUING EDUCATION, no. 45, Spring 1990 © Jossey-Bass Inc., Publishers and Liebowitz (1983) defined mentoring behaviorally as an integrative process. Mentors perform a variety of behaviors: teaching, guiding, advising, counseling, sponsoring, role modeling, validating, motivating, protecting, and communicating. Once a mentoring relationship has been initiated, the mentor provides the informal link between the student and the institution.

Much as the Proseminar is the keystone in the adult degree program of Ottawa University, the learning autobiography (LAB) is the hallmark of the course. As a course requirement, the LAB serves as an indicator of the level of writing skill a student possesses. It is a required assignment— required in the sense that to receive a course grade a student must complete the LAB along with other assignments.

The purposes of the LAB are to (1) provide an opportunity for the student to demonstrate writing ability; (2) provide an occasion for the student to reflect on and assess previous learning environs; (3) evaluate the student's strengths and weaknesses; (4) plan for future educational experiences; (5) assist the faculty adviser in participating in these educational experiences; and (6) build confidence, mutual respect, and trust in the student-adviser interaction. The assigned topics go much further than the demonstration of an ability to write coherent and cohesive paragraphs. A description of the topics indicates the breadth and depth of the learning autobiography.

1. *Formal education:* In your past, what educational experiences were most meaningful? Why? What have you learned about yourself as to the type of learner you are? In what type of situations do you learn best?

2. *Persons:* What persons have had the greatest impact on you as you experienced growth and development? Who were your "models" or "mentors" or who helped you develop a sense of direction?

3. *Significant events:* What significant incidents out of your past life experience contribute most to the kind of person you are today, your personal sense of direction, and the values you hold? What have you learned from these events?

4. *Informal learning, skills, and abilities:* What other educational experiences have you had outside the formal classroom setting that have contributed to your learning? What specific knowledge and skills have you gained from these experiences?

5. *Future goals:* What are your future goals—educational, professional, and personal? What things stand in the way of your accomplishing these goals?

6. *Philosophy:* What is your philosophy—those ideas, principles, values, or ideals that are most important to you as an individual?

These topics and corresponding particulars are simple in nature but provide the basis for a good mentoring relationship.

Shared knowledge and shared experiences are inherent in the student-mentor relationship. Students have ample opportunity to learn about the mentor. (At least, they should!) In a similar manner, the mentor must be able to relate to the experiences of the student. What is the suitable learning environment for Mary? What future aspirations does Jim have? Unlike traditional students, no two adult students have the same background. One student expressed this diversity well: "My life has not been extraordinary, but it is unique to me." The recognition of this "unique" person concept through the learning autobiography fosters mutual trust and respect. Mentors are able to comprehend the fact that it is not easy for an adult to return to the classroom after an absence of years, even decades. The natural fear and anxiety may be lessened by the knowledge that a mentor who appreciates and respects the individual as an "adult student"—a unique person—is present.

The procedures for completing the LAB are uncomplicated. At the first course session, the instructor furnishes the class with an outline of the topics. The handout given to the students outlines some aids that will provide assistance in writing the LAB. The use of a lifeline exercise with accompanying highs and lows is most appropriate. The "whys" and "wherefores" of the peaks and valleys are identified with particular time periods, events, or persons. The key words in this process are choose, describe, and reflect. Choose a particular happening, a phase in one's life, or a significant person who may have challenged one's previous values, ideas, or self-concepts. Next, describe what occurred. Concrete details give life to what may be an isolated happening. Then reflect on the importance of the experience. Stand back and consider the meaning of what has been chosen in terms of one's needs, aspirations, development, and ideals. Why has this person/event/experience been selected from all of the things that have occurred?

To further foster the mentoring relationship, it is important that the student feel that the assignment is beneficial beyond the value of "writing practice." Each instructor employs singular techniques to emphasize the worth of the exercise. Nonthreatening expressions are an integral part of the instructions; anonymous comments from previous LABs serve to indicate that others have completed the exercise and have done well. There is no "number of pages" obligation, nor is there any numerical count of persons, events, goals, and the like that are to be listed. This open-ended approach provides sufficient opportunity for the student to reflect as much as he or she deems suitable. Student responses, with few exceptions, have been gratifying and, at times, overwhelming. "Nothing of import" in my life becomes a LAB of great depth and merit. One student may

have given the appropriate definition to the LAB by stating in her introduction, "I moved from asking the question 'Why am I doing this?' to
'Why haven't I done this before?' " The value of the exercise can be
gleaned from additional student responses.

> During the course of the Proseminar, I wrote the required installments
> on my learning autobiography. I say *required* because I never would
> have accomplished such a task on my own initiative. I have never
> believed that such an undertaking would be beneficial. Now that the
> task is finished, I recognize the value. The fruit of such a task can
> never be discerned by one who merely sits down to read the finished
> product. The pages of the autobiography represent only the spring-
> board which gave momentum to many hours of contemplation, plan-
> ning, and resolution which could have meaning only to me. . . . This
> learning autobiography is an expression of a learning experience it-
> self. . . . From now on, as a result, my approach to learning will never
> be the same.

> Life is so busy that often I simply flow along in the stream, never
> taking the time to ponder the terrain already traveled and the journey
> still ahead. Yet it is important that the time be taken for this reflection.
> The greatest knowledge one can have, next to that of knowing God, is
> to know oneself. Who I am today, in a large measure, has been deter-
> mined by whom I have been in the past, where I have been, and with
> whom I have had contact.

Faculty place similar significance on the LAB in developing the
mentoring relationship. Each adult student has a personality that must
be recognized by the mentor in carrying out the various mentoring behaviors. Learning styles and strategies, good and bad educational experiences, events and persons, goals and philosophies give identities to adult
students and shape their development. As one student aptly observed,
"We bring an awful lot of 'baggage' to the classroom." A mentor is
mindful of this "baggage" and recognizes the importance of this part of
the total person and personality.

Further applications of the LAB are many. Two excellent opportunities for use are reentry programs and career counseling. Courses designed
to assist the adult student entering college for the first time or entering as
a returning student may consider the learning autobiography. The LAB
could be the core of the program since in the LAB students provide
insights into their educational and life experiences that are significant
and relevant for a successful college tenure. Learning styles, learning
environments, and learning preferences are only a few of the vital areas

of information that are gleaned from the LAB. With this knowledge, the advising process is facilitated and strengthened.

Many career counselors utilize a form of the LAB. "What do I know about myself" is the question frequently asked but seldom adequately answered. The LAB affords the respondent the means to develop in-depth answers to this question. Which experiences have been rewarding? Which experiences have been disappointing? What learning environment do I enjoy? Am I a "people" person? What skills do I have that are suitable for a given career? In replying to these queries, respondents become aware of the value of past experiences. Further, they provide "groundwork" for counselors to assist in the "search" for careers.

Daloz (1986) defines mentors as guides. They lead us along the journey of our lives. He advises, "In order to understand the mentor as a guide, however, it will be necessary to go back and look more closely at the journey itself. To do that, we consider the importance of 'story' as a way of making sense of life's changes, focusing on a particular kind of story—the journey tale" (pp. 17–18). In its adult degree program Ottawa University gives impetus to this mentoring relationship with the learning autobiography.

References

Daloz, L. A. *Effective Teaching and Mentoring: Realizing the Transformational Power of Adult Learning Experiences.* San Francisco: Jossey-Bass, 1986.

Lea, D., and Liebowitz, Z. B. "A Mentor: Would You Know One If You Saw One?" *Supervisory Management,* 1983, *28* (3), 32–35.

Callistus W. Milan is associate professor of education at the Phoenix Center of Ottawa University.

Learning to cope with stress is invaluable for the adult student.
Adult educators need to deal with this issue.

Stress, Coping, and Adult Education

Sybil A. McClary

From its introduction as a methodological concept in the early 1950s, stress has become a widely discussed topic in both academic and popular publications (Marsella, 1984). Interest in the topic has increased as evidence has accumulated linking stress to mental illness, heart disease, stroke, immune system response, and possibly cancer (Taylor, 1986). Both researchers and the general public are curious about what health problems are connected with the pressures involved in normal living. In addition, there has been increased interest in the relationship between stress in different age and gender groups and how that stress can result in decreased job satisfaction, loss of productivity, illness, and even death (Shermerhorn, Hunt, and Osborn, 1988; Matteson and Ivancevich, 1987).

Both the academic literature and the popular press appear to be publishing and writing more about stress. It is prevalent in commercial advertising for food, leisure, and fitness-related products. It is also the topic for many management seminars and employee assistance programs. Various popular reports are connecting stress to life-style and drug use as well as to specific diseases. It has become a major concept in explanations of human behavior and the general quality of life (Selye, 1976).

Because of the usefulness of stress as a measure for the level and amount of stimuli with which an individual contends (Marsella, 1984), it is a most appropriate approach to understanding more about how individuals deal with the challenges of life. Challenges of marriage, parenting, military tours of duty, and work with AIDS victims are only a sampling of the adult developmental tasks, situations, roles, and careers being considered in terms of stress theory and research.

With the proliferation of adult education programs and their focus on adult development, it seems natural to include them in this investigation of stress. When adults return to a traditional or a nontraditional learning environment, their ability to cope with frustration, pressure, conflict, and positive and negative life events (including environmental conditions) is often an important aspect of their success and reported satisfaction. To date, few systematic investigations of the role of stress in adult education or its relationship to adult development have been reported.

Malcolm Knowles's theory of adult education (Knowles, 1984; Feuer and Gerber, 1988) suggests that adults succeed in situations where they are highly motivated, where they can participate in the learning process, and where learning content has practical applications. In addition, according to Knowles, adults find an informal setting conducive to learning, want to know exactly what is expected of them, want opportunities to practice their newly learned skills, and want to have immediate feedback on their learning progress. While they are students, most of the adult learners are also full-time workers, family members (often heads of households and parents of dependent children), and members of religious, social, and civic organizations. These multiple roles and the concomitant developmental tasks provide a rich diversity of experience that is brought to the classroom, but they also add to the everyday life stress of individuals as students and as adults.

All of the frustrations, conflicts, pressures, and life events associated with these multiple roles and experiences are being confronted by the adult learner, along with the challenge of the academic curriculum. This constant reaction to stressors and stress can either contribute to the learning experience or detract from it. Stress can be intense enough to keep the adult student from ever succeeding, or it can be intense enough to motivate exceptional academic accomplishments. The consideration of stress as an ingredient in the adult learning and development process appears to be timely and necessary.

Those who plan and provide adult education programs and experiences can benefit from understanding how stress is conceptualized, what the research suggests about the effects of stress, and how successful coping occurs. From this information educators can design and incorporate appropriate strategies that help adult students cope with and manage the stress they experience. Having contributed to stress management, educators add one more dimension to the adult student's positive learning experience.

A summary of the existing theories of stress and some of the implications that information on stress and coping appears to have for adult education are presented here. Specific strategies that are responsive to existing information about stress include the following: (1) a program designed to allow for and be responsive to stress factors that influence students, (2) orientation sessions to acquaint students with the effects of stress and how it can be managed in the learning environment, (3) individualized programs of study based on a personal contract of commitment and intent, (4) integration of the program of study into the students' work and lives, recognizing that their education does not necessarily rank first in priority, (5) personal attention, advising, and mentoring, along with social support, and (6) provision of academic challenge and rigor for adults who are developmentally ripe for an intense educational experience.

A Major Health and Quality-of-Life Issue

"Stress is considered any event which strains or exceeds an individual's ability to cope" (Lazarus and Launier, 1978, p. 455). *Stressor* is a term used to refer to the source of stress. Stress may also be used to describe the state of the body when it is under the impact of stressors. *Coping* is the term used to describe the reaction the individual employs after the stressor has been experienced.

Sources of stress are divided into the major categories of frustration, conflict, pressure, positive and negative life events, and environmental factors. Naturally, some of these are experienced on a daily if not hourly basis. Others are experienced only once in a lifetime. The level of intensity of the sources of stress depends on many factors. Generally the individual copes with stress as a normal aspect of living. At times the stress becomes more intense than the individual can manage.

Selye's model of the general adaptation syndrome (GAS) is considered a useful explanation of the individual's encounter with stress (Bee, 1987, p. 315). In the first stage a general alarm is set off, the "shock" stage. During this period body temperature and blood pressure go down. This change is followed by the "countershock" stage, in which both temperature and blood pressure rise. During this phase adrenalin flow increases, pain-inhibiting neurotransmitters are produced, and blood-clotting and cholesterol retention are accelerated.

If resistance is not successful, the final stage occurs, exhaustion that can result in death. Few people die directly of stress. They die of the continued bodily reaction to stress or of diseases that attack the body when it is under stress.

Another model of stress focuses on the external sources of stress and how they influence physical health (Holmes and Rahe, 1976; Chiriboga and Cutler, 1980; Bee, 1987; Stevens-Long, 1988). The life events scales developed by Holmes and Rahe and Chiriboga and Cutler are lists of events such as marriage, death of a spouse, and a parking citation.

Respondents total the events they have experienced to see how their stress scores compare with norms for predicting physical illness.

It is important to note that not all stress is negative. Getting married or buying a new house is a stressor because it requires adjustment. In addition, it is important to note that each individual may rate events uniquely in terms of positiveness or negativeness. To make the assessment even more complicated, some individuals seek more stress and thrive on more accumulated life events than do others.

A third model of stress, discussed by Bee (1987) and Marsella (1984), attempts to show how stress is a function of internal personality, cognitive and biological factors, and external resources and supports. The outcome of stress is one of three possibilities: no change, psychosocial or psychological growth, or adverse health and emotional functioning. In this complicated model, both positive and negative psychological and sociological factors are considered. The results of stress are seen as neutral, positive, or negative. All models consider the body to have a specific reaction to life experience.

Coping is a concept that focuses on the conscious reactions an individual employs in response to stress. Coping can be divided into four types of techniques. The first is to physically remove the source of stress or escape from it. The second is to change one's perception of the stress so that the response is less intense. The third is to change the physiological state of the body so that the unconscious physical reactions are lessened (Rimm and Masters, 1979).

A fourth category of coping is the development of a healthy life-style that promotes the other coping techniques and eliminates other physical stresses on the body. Eating properly, maintaining appropriate weight, exercising, following medical treatment plans, and eliminating excessive use of alcohol, nicotine, and caffeine are suggested (Friedman and Booth-Kewley, 1987; Mathews, 1982). Learning to relax and using biofeedback techniques are also considered part of the wellness life-style.

As a part of understanding stress and coping, research has suggested particular characteristics are associated with a high risk for stress. The most notable characteristic is the type A personality. A person with a type A personality is competitive, rushed, driven, hostile, aggressive, and loud. This is considered a personality type in that it reflects habits of behavior developed over time. Research has shown that if a person expresses hostility in the form of verbal and physical aggression, he or she is more likely to have heart disease and a heart attack than are persons who do not display these characteristics.

Other internal factors involved in coping include the inherited ability to resist stress, cognitive abilities that contribute to creative problem solving, attitudes and values that allow the "reframing" of negatives into positives, and possibly developmental factors that foster coping.

Developmental issues related to stress and coping are speculative in that little significant research has been done and results are not conclusive. Bee (1987) attempts to summarize what she believes is of note in this area.

Research indicates that particular kinds of stressors are experienced as quite intense, at least for women. These stressors are referred to as the "exits" or losses that appear to reach their peak in middle age. They include the loss of a marriage to divorce, loss of children as they mature, and loss of parents at their death.

Existing research regarding age indicates that younger individuals report more negative assessments of particular life events than do older adults. They also report becoming obsessed over negative life events while older adults report being able to get over things more easily.

Because the adjustment to both positive and negative life events requires stress management or coping, Bee suggests that during the ages of entering and exiting many new roles, adults experience stress more than they do during the stages when roles are more stable. This would explain why younger adults who are entering many new roles as workers, spouses, and parents report more stress than do older adults who may not be experiencing role "exits."

Physiological research has shown that the ability to resist the impact of stress on the body diminishes as age increases (Bee, 1987; Stevens-Long, 1988). The alarm reaction takes longer for older adults, as does the resistance phase. During this latter phase the immune system is less resistant to disease attacking the body. With age, the body in general becomes less resilient, partly because of the damage the resistant stage of stress reaction has done over the years.

Experience and control of stressors are factors in one's ability to manage stress. Experience does come with age, but effective stress management often requires experience with specific stressors (Selye, 1976). No developmental research has shown experience to be a factor in how older people deal with stress. Also, control has not been investigated from a developmental perspective, but it can be considered relevant to the extent that older adults have the cognitive resources, material resources, and experience to have more control over the stressors in their lives.

Social support has been studied in a developmental perspective. Its relationship to stress has been shown in a number of studies (Bee, 1987). Having someone to talk with about the stressor appears to help with coping. It also has been shown that it is not just having friends but having intimate relationships with others that is crucial. Intimacy here means friends who listen and support personal feelings and concerns, and who are accessible whenever help is needed.

Social support appears to fluctuate with age. In the middle adult years, individuals report fewer friends than do twenty- to thirty-year-olds. With increasing age the support system decreases, and intimate friendships become more difficult to develop.

It is important to remember that individual differences in stress and coping remain the dominant theme in understanding stress theories. Developmental phases and stages may be one more input into a complex system of interacting factors that explain the stress process.

Relevance to Adult Education

Adult education has been designed to be responsive to the particular needs and characteristics of adults (Knowles, 1984). Developing these programs for traditional universities, nontraditional programs, and corporate training systems has been based on the belief that adults will grow and prosper academically in these specially designed learning environments. As new information is accumulated about the way adults deal with stress and subsequent illness, it becomes important to consider this aspect as a part of the development of adult education programs. As with any product in the market, new ideas need to be investigated and incorporated if the product is to keep up with the times.

If adult educators are really interested in a student-centered design for learning, it is important to consider stress. Because it is often a welcome stimulant for some individuals, stress can be productively used in the learning process. But because it also can overload some students, it must be dealt with in order to clear the way for learning.

The role of stress in physical health and quality of life must become a part of any adult learning program that purports to be aware of adult students in their larger context as workers, parents, and citizens. The general satisfaction of adult students with their learning experience is often one of our best measures of performance (if not our best recruitment method), which makes the role of stress in their lives an important factor. Stress, being a major factor in student satisfaction and learning success, must be a concern for adult educators.

Adult education programs are always looking for ways to improve. Not being tied to the traditions of their institutions, they are continuously assessing the curricula and implementation strategies in an attempt to ensure continued support by administrators and funders. Taking stress factors into consideration may show the willingness of program developers to meet new knowledge as it is accumulated. It may also model a willingness to put theory into practice, which has been a foundation of adult education. By designing strategies that have stress management as their focus, adult education programs demonstrate the attitudes of creativity and common sense, the very combination applauded by adult students.

Practical Implications for Programs

Program designers can begin by looking at their adult education programs from a new perspective. This perspective recognizes the importance of stress in the lives of adult students and attempts to redesign where necessary in an attempt to react to the accumulating information on stress and coping.

The development of a new telephone call reception system is a good example. When calls are received from current or prospective students, how many questions can be answered by the first person the caller reaches? Developing a knowledgeable receptionist who not only can answer many of the questions but also knows when and to whom to transfer the call can make a big difference to a busy caller who is looking for service, not complications.

In addition to looking at staff and administrative innovations designed to reduce the time and effort it takes adult students to move through the system, program designers may want to look at their instructional delivery system. Are courses offered in a variety of formats (weekly classes, independent study, weekend intensives, videotapes) so that students can take advantage of a format appropriate to their individual educational needs and time constraints? Are choices of instructors available? Variety in formats and contexts affords students the opportunity to match their needs at a particular time with program offerings. Control over their learning delivery system can help them with their stress management.

An orientation program or session on stress and coping can be an effective approach. By providing academic information on this relevant topic, program designers are able to help students understand their own stress and how the adult education program has been redesigned to help students in this regard. Combining the theory of stress with practical applications to their own learning environment shows students an important adult learning model. Assessment of personality type, life events, coping techniques, and life-style can be helpful. The teaching of relaxation and other coping techniques could also be included in the orientation. Hopefully, students will be able to apply stress theories to their home and work life as well as to their educational experience.

Individualized programs allow the student to design the combination of courses and learning experiences that they believe will most benefit them. These programs need to be limited by certain standards set by the program developers and accreditation bodies. However, the individualized program gives the student flexibility and control. It is responsive to the research, which suggests that stress is also individualized. Some seek out stress; others cannot handle much stress. Adding consideration of stress factors to the educational plan could be an important element in degree plans.

Designing these programs can create its own level of stress. This is where individualized advising is helpful.

Social support and intimate social relationships are considered coping resources. The adult student's adviser plays a crucial role in this process. The student should be encouraged to develop a personal, friendly relationship with advisers and instructors. There is no reason to maintain a formal distance between student and teacher or student and adviser. Assuming appropriateness and propriety, close relationships between students and advisers contribute to successful stress management. The discussion of career concerns, family issues, and even financial problems (all stressors) may be a necessary part of the relationship.

Students are better able to cope if they have access to their advisers or instructors when needed. The instructor's stress level needs to be considered as well, but easy accessibility increases the students' sense of control over their own educational processes. It also provides social support.

Students should be encouraged to find peers with whom they can talk about concerns and to whom they can turn when they need academic help or program advice. In addition, having a staff member who functions as a peer adviser is appropriate. The peer may be a student or former student in the program who can offer helpful advice on courses, study strategies, and coping techniques. By encouraging the student to broaden a personal network of social support, the level of coping can be increased.

Academic advisers who know and have a level of appropriate intimacy with their students can make the design of an individualized program less stressful and quite stimulating. Showing the student how to combine transfer courses, experiential learning, future coursework, and standardized exams into a degree program can be as exciting and gratifying as designing a dream house.

Getting the program of study into written form so that a personal commitment can be made by the student helps establish the structure and sense of security often desired. In this process, adult learners are not required to buy a lockstep program that someone else designed. Rather, they have a written, individual plan to refer to and be accountable for at the time of graduation.

Learning contracts, as Knowles describes them, can be made as well (Knowles and Associates, 1984). These written commitments are made at the beginning of each course or learning experience. They record the negotiated agreement between student and instructor for the course expectations and standards for evaluation. Learning contracts eliminate the potential for stressful conflicts if the student and the instructor later have differing perceptions of the learning objectives.

Integrating education into the adult's life begins by recognizing that the educational experience is one of many competing demands on the adult's time and resources. This has implications for dealing with stress.

The traditional view is that students should give education top priority. Adult educators generally recognize that this is unrealistic. As a part of the initial interview or orientation phase, students can be informed that time management is necessary in the education process. The time expected for study can be suggested to them so they can begin to readjust their current life roles. Helping students plan for this time relieves later stress. Discussion of this time commitment with significant others and employers is also necessary for successful time and stress management.

Allowing students to claim college credit for life and work experiences is an important element in many nontraditional programs. This is an example of the recognition by adult educators that education takes place in many contexts and that adults bring to the classroom a valuable set of roles and experiences that are not only enriching to classroom discussions but also actually equivalent to college credits. This supports the belief that education is and should be integrated with the life experience of students. It gives students a sense of worth and a potential boost to their educational goals. The defense of claims for credit is no easy task, but the stress involved in the writing activity is often energizing and stimulating, as it has the capacity to prove to the student as well as to the reviewers just how much students do know. This experience serves as an example of the positive role stress can have in stimulating a student's self-esteem.

Coursework can be designed to allow students to apply theory to practical problems in their work and lives. Allowing students to use projects accomplished in their work settings or communities as part of their coursework can be a valuable strategy for reducing stress. It connects their education to the real world and supports the notion that education is for life. It also increases motivation to do research and investigation. It can reduce stress by allowing individuals to be both employees and students at the same time. The integration of adult education into the work and leisure of the student helps to place value in lifelong learning. When something is valued, and therefore positively assessed, it is easier to cope with.

Personalized attention in both education and advising is important because it allows adult students to be in control of their own educational processes with professional help when necessary. With a professional available for advising and support, students are given a chance to compare their ideas with those of someone experienced in the process, thereby providing an opportunity for modeling. In this way the adult educator can build credibility by practicing what is preached. Healthy life-styles, attention to personal stress management, and the ability to build warm supportive relationships with students are important ingredients for modeling success. Having professional mentors who are able to guide and support adult students as they move through their unique educational programs builds a team that produces successful, satisfied students and instructors.

Challenge and rigor in the academic curriculum are essential. Knowles (1984) contends that adult students are highly motivated (in the middle adult years) and are also informed about what is being offered in traditional settings. They want the best of both worlds: academic challenge and credibility along with an approach that recognizes the role of stress in their lives.

The developmental theory expressed by Erikson, Levinson, and others (see Chapter One) suggests that developmental tasks associated with the adult students (ages twenty-five to fifty-five) include a desire for intimacy, motivation to ensure career competence, and motivation to be productive, all followed by periods of renewed creativity and vigor. This seems a perfect motivational context for academic challenge. Some of the stress associated with the life events of this period may be welcome and necessary for the energy and confidence the adult student needs to meet these developmental tasks. Stress management and healthy coping can only enhance the process by allowing students more energy for what they find more rewarding—the curriculum. With careful preparation and planning, the problems of negative stressors can be minimized.

Conclusion

Stress has become a popular and useful concept for both researchers and the public in understanding how individuals adjust to life events, developmental tasks, and subsequent life experiences. It has important implications for physical health and quality of life. It explains, in part, the disease process and shows how successful coping can be strategized.

The importance stress research and information have for adult education is considerable. The development of adult education programs that incorporate stress theories and stress management techniques will attract program support and increased numbers of students. Program design and implementation strategies need to be student centered and to reflect the nature of stress as both a positive and a negative experience for adult students. Educators need to capitalize on the positive by providing challenging academic programs that have relevance and applicability to the students' lives. Such programs help students cope with negative stressors by informing them about stress and specific stress management techniques.

Programs designed with stress theories taken into consideration might include personalized advising, individualized programs of study, support for building social support relationships with peers and professionals, programs of study integrated into the student's life and work, and opportunities to have instructors model effective coping and a generally healthy life-style.

Theories of stress and of adult education are based on the same assumption: Human behavior is not easily segmented into work, play, challenge, crisis, learning, teaching, stimulation, and alarm. Both sets of theories explain human behavior at a complex level of analysis. In doing so, they have applicability to everyday lives and have received a great deal of interest from the public. The application of both sets of theories benefits both the adult learner and the adult education programs.

References

Bee, H. L. *The Journey of Adulthood.* New York: Macmillan, 1987.

Chiriboga, D. A., and Cutler, L. "Stress and Adaptation: Life-Span Perspectives." In L. W. Poon (ed.), *Aging in the 1980s: Psychological Issues.* Washington, D.C.: American Psychological Association, 1980.

Feuer, D., and Gerber, B. "Uh-Oh . . . Second Thoughts About Adult Learning Theory." *Training,* 1988, pp. 31–39.

Friedman, H. S., and Booth-Kewley, S. "The Disease-Prone Personality: A Meta-Analytic View of the Construct." *American Psychologist,* 1987, *42,* 539–555.

Holmes, T. H., and Rahe, R. H. "The Social Readjustment Rating Scale." *Journal of Psychosomatic Research,* 1976, *11,* 213–218.

Knowles, M. S. *The Adult Learner: A Neglected Species.* (3rd ed.) Houston, Tex.: Gulf, 1984.

Knowles, M. S., and Associates. *Andragogy in Action: Applying Modern Principles of Adult Learning.* San Francisco: Jossey-Bass, 1984.

Lazarus, R. S., and Launier, R. "Stress-Related Transactions Between Person and Environment." In L. A. Pervin and M. Lewis (eds.), *Perspectives in Interactional Psychology.* New York: Plenum, 1978.

Marsella, A. J. "An Interactional Model of Psychopathology." In W. A. O'Connell and B. Lubin (eds.), *Ecological Approaches to Clinical and Community Psychology.* New York: Wiley, 1984.

Mathews, E. L. "Psychological Perspectives on the Type-A Behavior Pattern." *Psychological Bulletin,* 1982, *91,* 293–323.

Matteson, M. T., and Ivancevich, J. M. *Controlling Work Stress: Effective Human Resource and Management Strategies.* San Francisco: Jossey-Bass, 1987.

Rimm, D. C., and Masters, J. *Behavior Therapy.* (2nd ed.) New York: Academic Press, 1979.

Selye, H. *The Stress of Life.* New York: Knopf, 1976.

Shermerhorn, J. R., Hunt, J. G., and Osborn, R. N. *Managing Organizational Behavior.* New York: Wiley, 1988.

Stevens-Long, J. *Adult Life.* (3rd ed.) Mountain View, Calif.: Mayfield Publishing, 1988.

Taylor, S. E. "Adjustment to Threatening Events: A Theory of Cognitive Adaptation." *American Psychologist,* 1986, *38,* 1161–1173.

Sybil A. McClary is assistant professor of psychology at the Kansas City Center of Ottawa University.

A wealth of recent material is concerned with adult development.

Resources on Adult Development

Linda H. Lewis, Rosemary S. Caffarella

The previous chapters in this volume have focused on practical techniques by applying adult development theory to the learning environment. While major adult development concepts have been cited that describe stage theory as well as adults' physiological and cognitive development, no one resource can provide comprehensive coverage of the topic. Therefore, this final chapter is presented as a supplemental resource guide for individuals interested in further surveying the literature.

There are a plethora of journal articles, dissertations, and conference proceedings that explore every aspect of adult development. In addition, books, monographs, and research reports are available that provide overviews of developmental theories and chronicle adults' life experiences. Therefore, in determining what should be included in the listing, the first task was to delimit the scope of the resources.

The annotated bibliography in this chapter is a synopsis of books and monographs published in the past fifteen years. These works primarily address the psychosocial aspects of adult development, although some attention is devoted to physiological development. The selected references are distinctive among the many sources available by virtue of their readability, relevance, impact, and currency.

The resources in this chapter are divided into two major subsections: (1) generic literature on adult development and (2) women's development. The reasoning behind this division is that recent research suggests that

The authors thank Sandra L. Hastings, a graduate student at the University of Connecticut, for her invaluable assistance in the retrieval and review of resources identified in this chapter.

women's development patterns may be different from men's, and yet a significant portion of the generic literature still reflects research based primarily on white, middle-class, largely male samples. A second bias in the literature is a lack of investigations of the developmental patterns of various ethnic groups and socioeconomic classes. Thus, in reviewing the literature suggested, the contextual constraints of past research must be viewed with a critical eye.

Although we have focused this resource list on books and monographs, readers are encouraged to select from the wide array of resources, including numerous journals, to expand their understanding of development in adulthood. A representative sample of some of the major sources of research and articles on adult development are the following:

> *Adult Education Quarterly*
> *American Psychologist*
> *Development Psychology*
> *Educational Gerontology*
> *International Journal of Aging and Human Development*
> *Journal of Applied Physiology*
> *Journal of Marriage and Family*
> *Journal of Personality and Social Psychology*
> *Journal of Physical Education, Recreation, and Dance*
> *Medicine and Science in Sport and Exercise*
> *Perceptual and Motor Skills*
> *Psychology of Women Quarterly*
> *Psychology Today*

Those who are interested in reviewing literature beyond that annotated here should keep in mind that resources on adult development are categorized according to a variety of topic headings. Adulthood, aging, maturation, middle age, emotional maturity, and moral and cognitive development are useful descriptors to use when conducting a literature search. Our best to you if you choose to go further with this developmental journey.

Annotated Bibliography

Generic Literature

Barrow, G. *Aging, the Individual, and Society.* (4th ed.) New York: West, 1989.

This informative text utilizes a social problems approach to the study of gerontology. Social situations problematical or undesirable for a great number of the elderly as well as issues problematical for society at large are the central tenets of this work. Fieldwork suggestions, references, and resources are useful addenda.

Bee, H. L. *The Journey of Adulthood.* New York: Macmillan, 1987.
This volume provides a well-written and comprehensive overview of what the author terms the journey of adulthood. The way adults change or develop in both systematic and individual ways throughout the adult years is stressed. The beauty of the book is that the author writes to the reader in a very personal way about the subject of development, without losing the empirical and descriptive depth of the material.

Binstock, R., and Shanas, E. *Handbook of Aging and the Social Sciences.* New York: Van Nostrand Reinhold, 1985.
Developed for use by researchers, practitioners, policymakers, and students, this volume reviews aging from the perspective of various social sciences. A multidisciplinary approach is utilized to examine five perspectives: the social aspects of aging, aging and the social structure, aging and the social systems, aging and interpersonal behavior, and aging and social intervention.

Birren, J. E., and Schaie, K. W. *Handbook of the Psychology of Aging.* (2nd ed.) New York: Van Nostrand Reinhold, 1985.
This gerontological handbook presents up-to-date research in the psychology of aging and is especially useful to professionals working with the aged. A cultural context is utilized to examine environmental and health influences on aging and behavior. Stress, disease, and changes in personality, memory, and perception are some of the topics discussed in this guide.

Birren, J. E., and Sloane, R. B. (eds.). *Handbook of Mental Health and Aging.* Englewood Cliffs, N.J.: Prentice-Hall, 1980.
This comprehensive text reviews the theory, research, and current practice of mental health and aging. Contributors to this volume address treatment procedures for adult behavior as well as the impact of biological and environmental influences on the aging process. Major areas covered include current social issues, genetics, learning, memory, personality adjustment, environment, depression, sexuality, relaxation, and exercise.

Bridges, W. *Transitions: Making Sense of Life's Changes.* Reading, Mass.: Addison-Wesley, 1980.
This short and highly readable volume provides a very clear and understandable overview of the process of transitions in adulthood. Interweaving literature, anthropological notions of development, and personal

experiences, the author describes three major phases of the transition process: the endings, the neutral zone, and the new beginnings. In addition, he gives some very useful self-help suggestions for how to move through each of the described phases.

Erikson, E. H. (ed.). *Adulthood.* New York: Norton, 1978.

How maturity is envisioned and experienced, particularly by males in various cultures and diverse religious traditions, is the subject of this collection of essays. The book is a much-needed antidote to the prevalence of the American, white, Anglo-Saxon male perspective found in much of the literature.

Erikson, E., Erikson, J., and Kivnick, H. Q. *Vital Involvement in Old Age.* New York: Norton, 1987.

Presented in this book are interviews with twenty-nine octogenarians to determine the success today's elderly have in attaining a balance between integrity and despair, as defined by Erikson. These personal accounts enhance our understanding of old age. Active involvement in life surfaces as a key component for successful aging.

Gould, R. L. *Transformations: Growth and Change in Adult Life.* New York: Simon & Schuster, 1978.

This popular book focuses on the "concerns and changing patterns of self-awareness" that occur in men and women between the ages of sixteen and fifty. Gould postulates that growth toward autonomy is achieved when individuals continue to challenge their beliefs about their postures in relationship to parents, significant others, and their own growth processes.

Hayslip, B., Jr., and Panek, P. E. *Adult Development and Aging.* New York: Harper & Row, 1989.

This volume has broad-based appeal for readers with diverse academic backgrounds. Research and theory, balanced by the applied aspects of adulthood and aging, are topically organized. Charts and graphs strengthen key points, and a substantial bibliography enhances the content.

Hitchcock, A. A., and Nott, W. L. (eds.). *Midlife Change: An Annotated Bibliography.* Falls Church, Va.: National Vocational Guidance Association, 1981.

This in-depth overview for both researchers and practitioners addresses theoretical issues and the implications for practice in career counseling and education. (Available from National Vocational Guidance

Association, 2 Skyline Place, Suite 400, 5203 Leesburg Pike, Falls Church, Virginia 22041.)

Hultsch, D. F., and Duetsch, F. *Adult Development and Aging: A Life-Span Perspective.* New York: McGraw-Hill, 1981.

This text examines adulthood from a life-span perspective. Emphasis is given to theories that explicate the life transitions and life events that frame an individual's contextual development.

Kalish, R. A. *Late Adulthood: Perspectives on Human Development.* (2nd ed.) Pacific Grove, Calif.: Brooks/Cole, 1982.

This short volume is very readable and provides a useful overview of adult development in the later years. Topics addressed include basic processes of aging; physical and mental health; personality and roles; practical issues of money, retirement, and the living environment; and community responses to older persons.

Kegan, R. *The Evolving Self: Problems and Process in Human Development.* Cambridge, Mass.: Harvard University Press, 1982.

Kegan creatively interprets Piagetian theory to propose a new framework for understanding the developmental process. He concludes that "meaning-making," or the drawing and redrawing of the distinction between self and others, is due to the human need to be simultaneously autonomous from yet connected to others. Accordingly, the book emphasizes the stages of transformation during the adult years, offering alternative intervention techniques.

Kimmel, D. C. *Adulthood and Aging.* New York: Wiley, 1980.

The central theoretical framework posited in this text states that the dynamic interplay between change and consistency is a central characteristic of development during adulthood. Intended to raise the awareness of issues related to growing old in a changing society, perspectives of early theorists are included.

Knox, A. B. *Adult Development and Learning: A Handbook on Individual Growth and Competence in the Adult Years.* San Francisco: Jossey-Bass, 1977.

This classic work synthesizes the findings of more than one thousand early studies in adult learning and development for educators and helping professionals to facilitate the design of planned, proactive services specific to individual needs. Knox identifies the following in his study: the circumstances that promote adult learning; learning abilities over the life span; and the impact of family roles, social activities, education, occupation, personality characteristics, and health on development and learning.

Krupp, J. A. *Adult Development: Implications for Staff Development.* Colchester, Conn.: Rise, 1981.

This monograph clearly and concisely explicates the stages of adult development. Definitive suggestions for the staff development of educators are offered based on the general characteristics identified in each stage.

Levinson, D. J., Darrow, D. N., Klein, E. B., Levinson, M. H., and McKee, B. *The Seasons of a Man's Life.* New York: Ballantine Books, 1978.

This volume is one of the best-known studies of adult development. Levinson's theoretical perspective of middle adulthood years defines a universal male developmental cycle based on an in-depth study of forty men between the ages of thirty-five and forty-five. The book identifies developmental tasks related to each period and describes the various approaches utilized by this diverse population.

Maddox, G. H., and others (eds.). *Encyclopedia of Aging.* New York: Springer, 1987.

As a major reference for the period of later adulthood, this work offers concise, authoritative explanations for concepts related to the aging process. Approximately five hundred articles written by prominent scholars are featured in addition to one of the most comprehensive bibliographies in adult development literature.

Merriam, S. B. *Themes of Adulthood Through Literature.* New York: Columbia University Press, 1983.

In contrast to books that present compilations of research on adulthood, this unique volume promotes an understanding of adult development and aging through literature. Through the use of fictional selections, concepts that epitomize real-life encounters with the basic themes and issues of adulthood are brought to life. Poems, short stories, and excerpts from novels and plays illuminate major periods and central issues in adults' lives. Short essays that precede literary sections provide an organizational framework, while literary selections enable readers to relate the readings to their own individual life experiences.

Merriam, S. B. *Adult Development: Implications for Adult Education.* Columbus, Ohio: ERIC Clearinghouse on Adult, Career, and Vocational Education, 1984.

This concise monograph synthesizes the literature of adult development and offers application suggestions for educators and practitioners. The following sections are included: an overview of adult development; a description of the major sequential models and transition models of development; a description of the relationship between adult development and adult education; and practical applications in program development, instruction, and counseling.

Perlmutter, M., and Hall, E. *Adult Development and Aging*. New York: Wiley, 1985.

Designed as a classroom text, Perlmutter and Hall's work is an example of an interdisciplinary approach to adult development. They approach development from four different perspectives: the biological, the psychological, the sociological, and the cultural. The authors describe the more classical work in the field and integrate a number of human interest stories into the text.

Rice, F. P. *Adult Development and Aging*. Newton, Mass.: Allyn & Bacon, 1986.

This book presents an eclectic approach to adult development. That development occurs throughout the life span and that life demands change and adaptation are emphasized. Graphs, charts, and real-life examples abound.

Rogers, D. *The Adult Years*. Englewood Cliffs, N.J.: Prentice-Hall, 1979.

Designed as a classroom text, Rogers's work is an example of the human interest approach to the delivery of adult learning theory. She assesses the significance of current changes in adult life-styles, offers recommendations for future research, and suggests several societal changes that might redirect the study of adulthood.

Schaie, K. W. (ed.). *Longitudinal Studies of Adult Psychological Development*. New York: Guilford Press, 1983.

This significant work is a collection of seven longitudinal studies in the field of adult development. It is an important resource for educators as well as practitioners interested in gerontology.

Schaie, K. W., and Geiwitz, J. *Readings in Adult Development and Aging*. Boston: Little, Brown, 1982.

This anthology provides a balanced selection of readings representative of current scholarly inquiry in the field of adult development for educators and practitioners.

Schaie, K. W., and Willis, S. L. *Adult Development and Aging*. (2nd ed.) Boston: Little, Brown, 1986.

This very readable, comprehensive overview of the psychology of adult development and aging is based on documented longitudinal and cross-sectional studies. Behavioral aging in the context of biological and societal changes is examined in relation to the major theoretical models of adult development. Each chapter provides an annotated bibliography of related references as well as a summary of a recent research project.

Schlossberg, N. K. *Counseling Adults in Transition.* New York: Springer, 1984.

This practical guide introduces a theory of transition to explain the factors that affect the ability of individuals to cope with trigger events or nonevents in the adulthood years. The primary purpose of the text is to acquaint educators and practitioners with the need to integrate knowledge of adult development with process skills to effectively assist individuals in coping with change.

Sheehy, G. *Passages: Predictable Crises of Adult Life.* New York: Bantam Books, 1976.

This readable best-seller chronicles the predictable transitions of young and middle adulthood. Narratives of the lives of women and men illustrate gender similarities and differences in the developmental process. The book examines the variety of stage-related crises many couples experience.

Sheehy, G. *Pathfinders.* New York: Bantam Books, 1981.

This research identifies the universal characteristics of individuals able to sustain a sense of well-being in spite of transitions and obstacles. Material is presented to encourage readers to transform their own similar obstacles into opportunities for further personal growth and greater happiness.

Smelser, N. J., and Erikson, E. H. (eds.). *Themes of Work and Love in Adulthood.* Cambridge, Mass.: Harvard University Press, 1980.

The outcome of a 1977 interdisciplinary conference concerning central issues in the study of adult development, this volume is an excellent starting point for independent learners. In speculative essays eleven scholars, including Erikson, Gould, Levinson, and Lowenthal, encapsulate research results while tracing the roots of their theoretical perspectives.

Sugarman, L. *Life-Span Development Concepts, Theories, and Interventions.* New York: Methuen, 1986.

This volume provides a very comprehensive and yet concise empirically based description of the life-span perspective of development. The physical, cognitive, personality, and personal changes that occur over the life course are reviewed. A clear summary is also given of the life-events paradigm of development. The book concludes with a set of suggested interventions for promoting and facilitating development over the life span.

Turner, J. S., and Helms, D. B. *Contemporary Adulthood*. Chicago: Holt, Rinehart & Winston, 1989.

As an introductory text, this volume provides uniform coverage of the stages of young, middle, and late adulthood. Death, dying, and bereavement are covered extensively. In addition, the text format is easily adapted to either a chronological or a topical approach to adult development.

Vaillant, G. E. *Adaptation to Life*. Boston: Little, Brown, 1977.

This is a particularly well-written account of a fascinating longitudinal study of adult development in males. Described in the volume is a study of ninety-five men who were considered "the best and the brightest" during their undergraduate days. Utilizing psychoanalytical constructs, the investigators traced the response of these men to work and family responsibilities. The results challenge the assumption that personality is inalterably formed during the first five years of life.

Van Hoose, W. H., and Worth, M. R. *Adulthood in the Life Cycle*. Dubuque, Iowa: Brown, 1982.

A well-written overview of adulthood, this volume serves as an excellent introductory text to the subject. The book contains six major topic areas: stages in adulthood, physical and intellectual development, roles and relationships, the gender experience, mental health, and aging and death.

Wolman, B. B. (ed.). *Handbook of Developmental Psychology*. Englewood Cliffs, N.J.: Prentice-Hall, 1982.

This is a collection of fifty definitive literature reviews concerning physiological, social, and psychological development from infancy through old age. The section on adulthood includes overviews of research related to motherhood, fatherhood, adult sexual development, divorce, and work-life development.

Women's Development

Baruch, G., Barnett, R., and Rivers, C. *Lifeprints: New Patterns of Love and Work for Today's Women*. New York: McGraw-Hill, 1983.

A substantive investigation of the sources of well-being for 238 women, aged thirty-five to fifty-five, this volume explicates the emerging patterns of intimacy and work for contemporary American women. Women in various roles were studied to determine pleasures, problems, conflicts, and issues that affect the attainment of a sense of fulfillment.

Belenky, M. F., Clinchy, B. M., Goldberger, N. R., and Tarule, J. M. *Women's Way of Knowing*. New York: Basic Books, 1986.

This work is significant because it challenges the universal applicability of Perry's construct of intellectual reasoning. The quest for self and voice is identified as the central theme—"women's way of knowing." Based on research collected from 135 women, an epistemology with five different perspectives of women is presented.

Coles, R., and Coles, J. H. *Women of Crises: Lives of Struggle and Hope*. New York: Delta/Seymour, 1978.

This work brings alive the sociocultural perspective of adulthood by providing naturalistic, poetic, and inspiring portrayals of the lives of five women: a migrant worker, a black housewife, a Mexican-American cleaning women, an Eskimo wife and mother, and Caucasian maid. *Women of Crisis II*, a subsequent volume by the same publisher, depicts, again in depth, five additional lives of women in the same realistic and yet poetic style.

Fuchs, E. *The Second Season: Life, Love and Sex for Women in the Middle Years*. Garden City, N.Y.: Anchor Press, 1978.

As a "cultural and physiological examination of middle-aged women," this book is the work of an anthropologist. The author compares the experience of menopause in several different cultures and argues that menopause is a difficult experience for women in cultures in which competence-building role options are not always available.

Gilligan, C. *In a Different Voice*. Cambridge, Mass.: Harvard University Press, 1982.

With this ground-breaking research, Gilligan contests the concept of a universal standard of moral development, arguing that the male norm is an inappropriate basis for the explanation of women's ethical and moral reasoning. She identifies a "different voice" that is descriptive of women's experiences but is absent in the construction of theory.

Josselyn, R. *Finding Herself: Pathways to Identity Development in Women*. San Francisco: Jossey-Bass, 1987.

This longitudinal study of eleven women illuminates the psychosocial differences in women's development. The author defines four approaches that women choose in making decisions about family and children, careers, religion, relationships, and world view.

Rogers, N. *Emerging Woman.* Point Reyes, Calif.: Personal Press, 1980.

A personal journey of one woman and her development during the life cycle. Her dichotomous needs of autonomy and correctedness are examined in relation to her evolving ideas about self, men, and relationships.

Rubin, L. B. *Women of a Certain Age: The Mid-Life Search for Self.* New York: Harper & Row, 1979.

In this short, readable work, Rubin realistically appraises the paradoxical changes of 160 midlife women. The findings dispel some of the myths associated with midlife transition and underscore women's issues and significant milestones in women's lives.

Spencer, A. *Seasons.* New York: Paulist Press, 1982.

This concise, easy-to-read book contrasts the development of women and men utilizing Levinson's theoretical framework. Factors prohibiting ego autonomy for women are examined. The concluding section presents a valuable overview of the important theories in the literature concerning the psychology of women.

Linda H. Lewis is associate professor of adult and human resources education at the University of Connecticut.

Rosemary S. Caffarella is associate professor of educational studies at the Virginia Commonwealth University.

INDEX

ORDERING INFORMATION

NEW DIRECTIONS FOR ADULT AND CONTINUING EDUCATION is a series of paperback books that explores issues of common interest to instructors, administrators, counselors, and policy makers in a broad range of adult and continuing education settings—such as colleges and universities, extension programs, businesses, the military, prisons, libraries, and museums. Books in the series are published quarterly, in Fall, Winter, Spring, and Summer, and are available for purchase by subscription as well as by single copy.

SUBSCRIPTIONS for 1990 cost $42.00 for individuals (a savings of 20 percent over single-copy prices) and $56.00 for institutions, agencies, and libraries. Please do not send institutional checks for personal subscriptions. Standing orders are accepted.

SINGLE COPIES cost $12.95 when payment accompanies order. (California, New Jersey, New York, and Washington, D.C., residents please include appropriate sales tax.) Billed orders will be charged postage and handling.

DISCOUNTS FOR QUANTITY ORDERS are available. Please write to the address below for information.

ALL ORDERS must include either the name of an individual or an official purchase order number. Please submit your order as follows:
    Subscriptions: specify series and year subscription is to begin
    Single copies: include individual title code (such as CE1)

MAIL ALL ORDERS TO:
    Jossey-Bass Inc., Publishers
    350 Sansome Street
    San Francisco, California 94104